LEATHERWORK

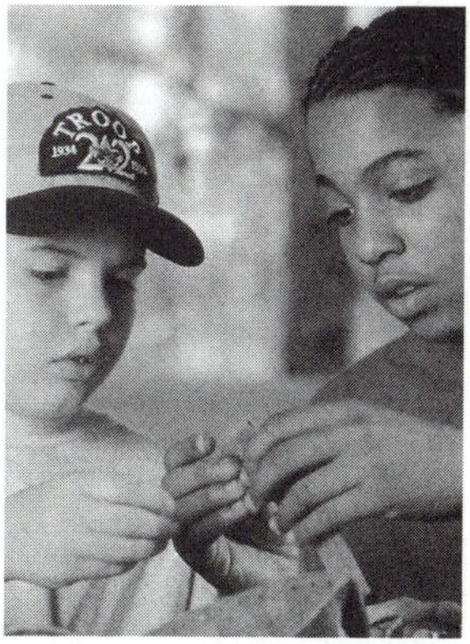

BOY SCOUTS OF AMERICA
IRVING, TEXAS

Requirements

1. Identify and demonstrate to your counselor the safe use of leatherworking tools. Show correct procedures for handling leathercraft dyes, cements, and finishes. Know first aid for cuts, internal poisoning, and skin irritation.
2. Explain to your counselor
   a. Where leather comes from
   b. What kinds of hides are used to make leather
   c. What are five types of leather
   d. What are the best uses for each type of leather
3. Make one or more articles of leather that use at least five of the following steps:
   a. Pattern layout and transfer
   b. Cutting leather
   c. Punching holes
   d. Carving or stamping surface designs
   e. Applying dye or stain and finish to the project
   f. Assembly by lacing or stitching
   g. Setting snaps and rivets
   h. Dressing edges
4. Recondition or show that you can take proper care of your shoes, a baseball glove, a saddle, furniture, or other articles of leather.
5. Do ONE of the following:
   a. Learn about the commercial tanning process. Report about it to your merit badge counselor.
   b. Tan the skin of a small animal. Describe the safety precautions you will take and the tanning method that you used.
   c. Braid or plait an article out of leather or vinyl lace.
   d. Visit a leather-related business. This could be a leathercraft supply company, a tannery, a leather goods or shoe factory, or a saddle shop. Report on your visit to your counselor.

33310A
ISBN 0-8395-3310-1

2003 Printing

Contents

Welcome to the World of Leatherwork 5
Safety and First Aid 7
All About Leather 11
Making Articles Out of Leather 15
Leather Care 75
Leather Tanning 79
Leather-Related Businesses 85
Glossary 87
Leathercraft Resources 89

Welcome to the World of Leatherwork

From the beginning of civilization to today's high-tech world, leather has served and enriched the lives of humans in many ways. No other natural material offers such variety and quality.

Whether you are interested in creating pictures in leather or making articles to be used or worn—including belts, footwear, wallets, sporting equipment, horse gear, historic reenactment garments, armor, sheaths, holsters, drums, and pouches—leather is one of the most versatile and long-lasting materials known. It can be molded, shaped, decorated, laced, stitched, glued, sewn, colored, and finished in many different ways.

As you complete the requirements to earn the Leatherwork merit badge, you will explore leather's history and its endless uses. You will learn to make a useful leather item using the same types of raw materials that your ancestors used, and you will be challenged to master skills like hand-stitching, lacing, and braiding. You will learn how to preserve and protect leather items so they will last your lifetime and beyond.

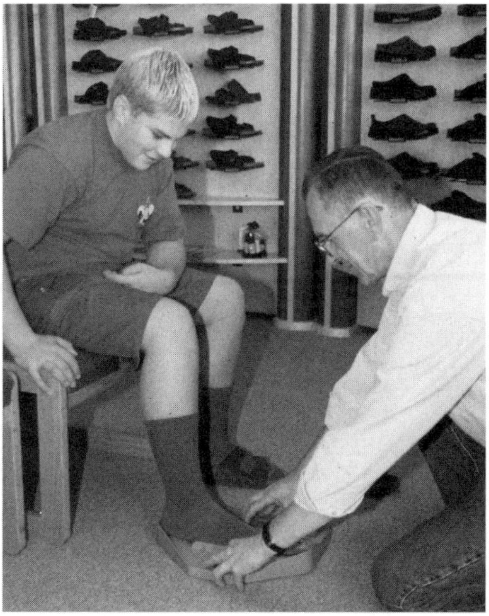

As you practice the leather-working techniques required for the merit badge, you are encouraged to use your creativity and imagination, and most of all, have FUN!

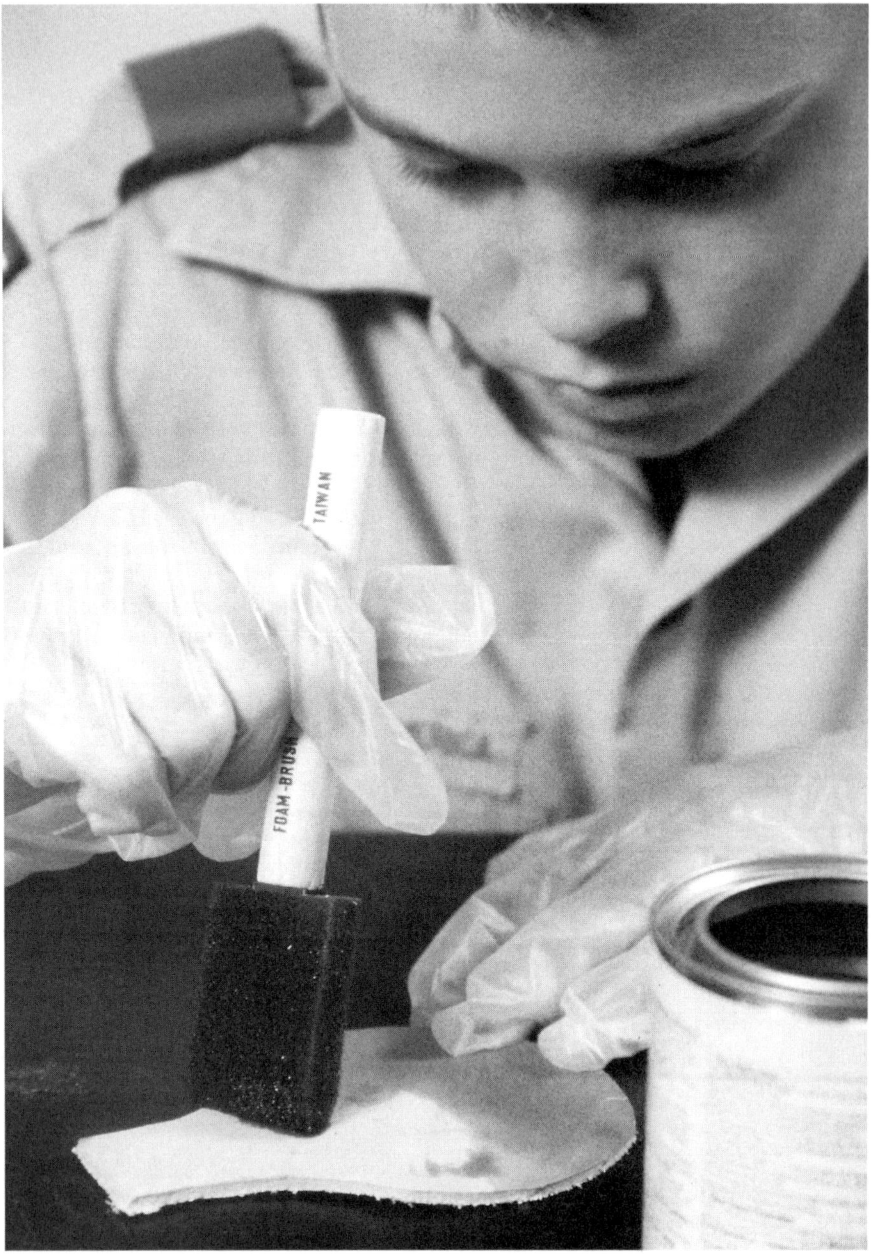
TAIWAN

Safety and First Aid

Many tools used in leatherworking have sharp cutting edges. They can be grouped into three major categories, depending on how they are used:

- Tools that are pushed (edgers, gouges, skivers, and some knives)
- Tools that are pulled (swivel knives, utility knives, groovers, and strap cutters)
- Tools that are struck (punches and chisels)

Make sure your tools are sharp—a dull cutting tool is dangerous. Grip them firmly to ensure complete control. Never put any part of your body in the path of a cutting edge.

Many dyes, cements, and finishes used in leatherworking contain hazardous chemicals. To safely use these materials, work in a well-ventilated area. Carefully read and follow all label instructions and warnings. Never ingest these chemicals or allow them to come in contact with skin. Protect your hands by wearing rubber gloves. Replace caps and lids to avoid spills. Never use chemicals near an open flame. Have a doctor or emergency medical service telephone number handy in case of an emergency.

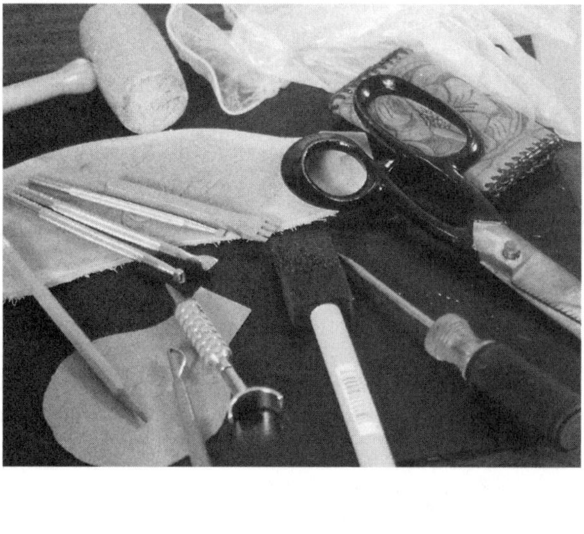

First-Aid Practices

To help ensure that your experience in working with leather will be both safe and fun, review the basic first aid instructions given below before beginning to work with leather.

Cuts and Scratches

Cuts and scratches are wounds—openings in the skin and tissues that can allow germs to enter the body and cause infection.

Puncture wounds can be dangerous because they allow germs into a wound that is hard to clean.

Remember, anyone suffering a serious wound should be treated for shock and seen by a physician immediately.

HOW TO TREAT

For minor scratches and cuts:

- Wash the wound with soap and water.
- Apply antiseptic to help prevent infection.
- Keep the wound clean by covering it with an adhesive bandage.

For larger cuts:

- Apply direct pressure to stop bleeding.
- Clean the wound as much as possible to limit infection.
- Cover an open wound with a sterile gauze pad or clean cloth folded into a pad. Hold the pad in position with tape, a cravat bandage, or other binder.

For puncture wounds:

- Encourage the wound to bleed to help remove anything that might have been forced inside.
- Use sterilized tweezers to pull out splinters, bits of glass, or other objects you can see.
- Wash the area with soap and water, apply a sterile bandage, and see a doctor.

Skin Irritation

Some dyes, cements, and finishes may cause redness, a burning sensation, itching, or swelling if they come into contact with skin.

HOW TO TREAT

- Wash the affected area with soap and water.
- Seek medical attention immediately if the irritation continues.

Internal Poisoning

Poisoning is the most frequent cause of accidental death among young children. They will swallow almost anything, including the chemicals used in leatherworking, so store such materials well out of their reach.

Symptoms of poisoning include nausea, stomach pains, vomiting, burns around the mouth, and erratic breathing. Often the most important sign of poisoning is the presence of the poison—open bottles, spilled chemicals, or other evidence of what might have been swallowed.

HOW TO TREAT

- Immediately find a telephone, taking any poison containers you find along with you.
- Call the poison control center toll-free at 800-222-1222, the local emergency center at 9-1-1, or an operator, and follow the instructions you are given.
- Treat the victim for shock and monitor breathing.
- Do not give anything by mouth unless you are told to do so by medical professionals.

See the *First Aid* merit badge pamphlet for more information on treating injuries.

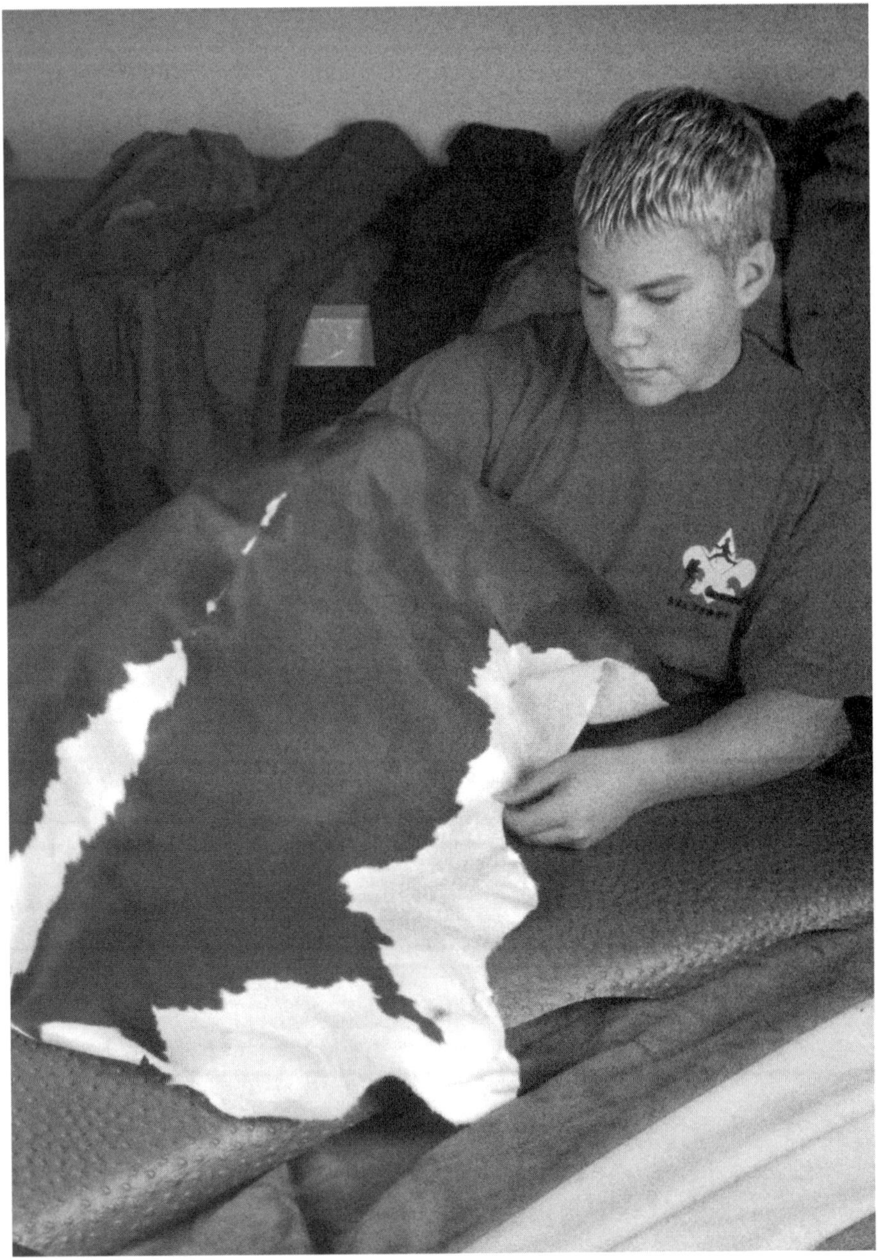

All About Leather

Leather—the tanned skin of an animal—is one of humankind's oldest and most serviceable materials. It was in common use when recorded history began, and it has remained important in the advance of civilization to the present day. Even now, with plastics and synthetic fibers in growing use, leather is still vital in our lives.

The animals that leather comes from may be grouped into two categories: domestic animals and wild or game animals.

Domestic Animals. The most commonly used leathers come from domestic or commercially raised animals. Most are by-products of the meat packing industry. Cows, pigs, and sheep provide the majority of leather product used today.

Wild or Game Animals. Wild or game animals such as deer, elk, moose, bison, and kangaroo also provide skins for leather-working use. Some are raised commercially, but most are taken in the wild by hunters who must follow federal and state laws designed to ensure the animals' continued survival. Exotic animals, including frogs, fish, turtles, snakes and other reptiles, and some birds, also provide skins for leatherworking, but their use is limited because of their declining populations, environmental concerns, and expense.

Leather thickness is measured in ounces. One ounce is equal to 1/64 inch in thickness. Thus, a weight of 16 ounces means the leather is 16/64 inch (or 1/4 inch) thick. Because the thickness of leather varies throughout the hide, leathers usually are described as having a range of thickness, such as 6 to 7 ounces.

Types and Uses of Leather

Many kinds of leather are available for leatherwork. Each has its own special qualities and best uses. For instance, the way leather has been tanned can determine how it is used.

Vegetable tanned leather (leather that has been tanned with extracts from tree bark) normally is used for items that call for a stiff, firm leather. It is the only leather that can be tooled.

Chrome tanned leather (leather that has been tanned with chemicals that contain chromium salts) normally is used for items that call for a soft, extremely flexible leather. It cannot be tooled.

Leather can be purchased in complete hides or skins. One of the more common leathers, cowhide, normally is sold in half-skins, called *sides.* Common types of leather and their uses are listed here to help you select a leather for a project.

Buffalo—The most common buffalo leather is Asian water buffalo. It comes in hides up to 40 square feet and features the bovine properties of cowhide and a coarse grain similar to pigskin. It is used for shoes, boots, and small leather goods.

Calfskin—This leather is taken from a young bovine in sides or whole hide up to 18 square feet. Is has a very tight grain and fine texture. Calfskin is used for shoes, boots, and fine leather goods.

Cowhide—The most common and versatile leather. It is usually tanned in sides of 18 to 24 square feet. Durable and easy to work with, cowhide can be up to 16 ounces thick, vegetable or chrome tanned. It is used for footwear, furniture, car upholstery, saddles, tack, handbags, and belts.

Deerskin—Tanned in whole hides of 7 to 12 square feet, deerskin is very soft and stretchy. Its light weight makes it ideal for gloves, moccasins, or garments.

Goatskin—Tanned in small, thin whole hides, this tough and durable leather often is finished in bright colors. It is used for women's shoes and the tops of cowboy boots.

Kangaroo—Thin and lightweight, but very durable, kangaroo leather is stronger weight-for-weight than any other leather. Whole skins average 5 to 7 square feet. Kangaroo is used for soccer shoes and sport gloves or is cut into thin strips for lacing and braiding.

Pigskin—Whole hides, 10 to 20 square feet, have a coarse grain texture and may be embossed with a texture to hide the grain or sueded and used as garment or lining leather. It is used for shoe linings, small leather goods, and garments.

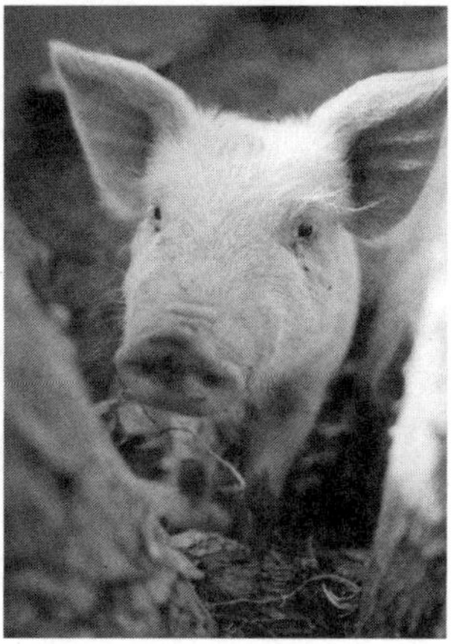

Reptile—Reptile leathers include snake, lizard, alligator, and crocodile. Available in whole hides or pieces in a variety of grains and textures, reptile is used for fancy leather goods, boots, shoes, belts, wallets, and handbags.

Sheepskin—Lightweight and delicate, the soft tannage makes nice garment leather. It is often tanned with the wool on as *shearling*. Sheepskin is used for coats, seat covers, and saddle lining.

Collecting Leather Samples

For requirement 2c, which asks you to explain five types of leather to your counselor, you may want to use this helpful leather sample label. The requirement will be more fun if you collect samples of the five types of leather, and this label will help you stay organized as you gather your samples and record their descriptions.

You can find leather samples at craft and leathercraft retail stores, saddleries, upholsterers, tanneries, shoe repair shops, farm and ranch suppliers, pet stores, and on the Internet (with your parent's permission and assistance).

Leather Sample Label

____

Type of leather

____

Tannage (vegetable, chrome, etc.)

____

Thickness characteristics

Uses: ______________________________

____

____

____

Making Articles Out of Leather

Before you can make articles out of leather, you must set up a suitable workspace and gather the necessary tools. The range of leatherworking techniques will grow with each step you take toward completing the project.

Setting Up a Safe Work Space

There are two very important things to consider when setting up the work space:

1. Make sure the area is well-lit. A good setup is overhead fluorescent lighting combined with clamp-on, swing-arm fixtures that can be positioned over the project.
2. Make sure the area is well-ventilated. The dyes, cements, and finishes that are used in leatherworking may give off strong, harmful fumes.

You will also need a sturdy table or workbench to be used as a:

1. Design and assembly area
2. Cutting area
3. Carving and stamping area
4. Dyeing, staining, and finishing area

General Leatherworking Tools and Supplies

Become acquainted with these **general leatherworking tools.** In some cases, ordinary tools used at home or school may be substituted.

Tools for Beginning the Project

Pencil, Paper, and Cardboard. Use a pencil and paper to draw projects as well as any designs for decorating them. Use cardboard to make reusable templates.

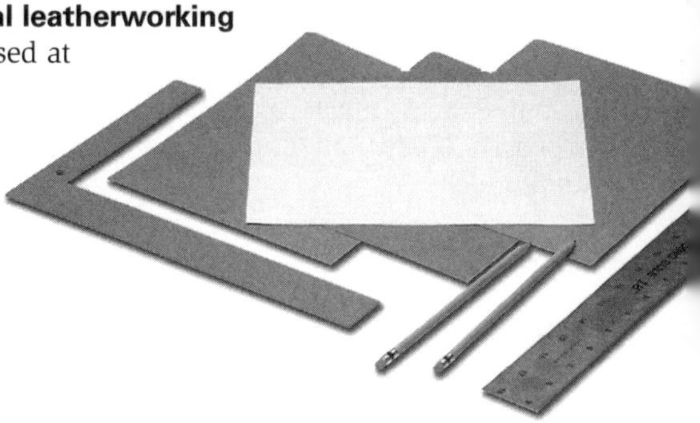

Ruler, Straight Edge, or Steel Square. Use these for measuring, pattern and design layout, and for cutting straight lines. Avoid unpainted steel rulers and squares because they will stain leather; ones made of aluminium, plastic, or wood work best.

Scratch Awl. Use for marking the outlines of cutting patterns and to mark the positions of holes for snaps, rivets, stitching, and lacing. Any awl with a sharp point—even an ice pick—will work. (Be sure to cover the point with a rubber guard when not in use.)

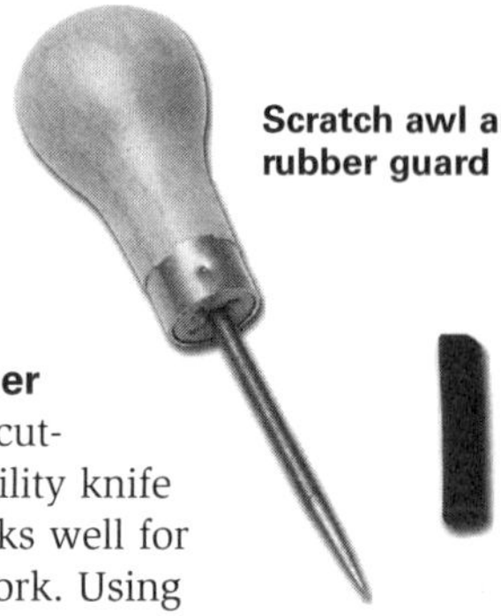

Scratch awl and rubber guard

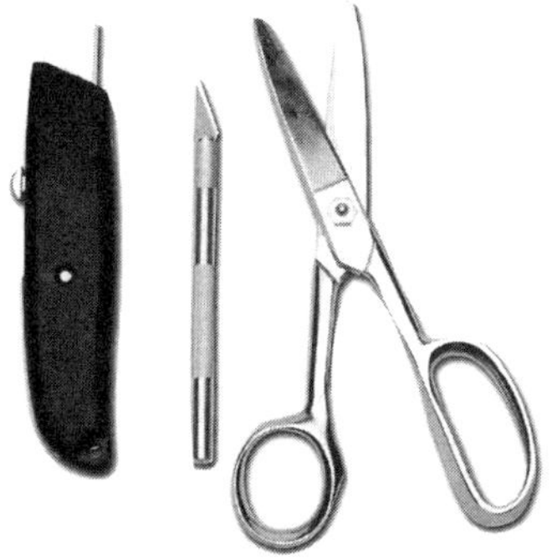

Knife and Leather Shears. Use for cutting leather. A utility knife or box knife works well for general leatherwork. Using snap-off blades will ensure a sharp cutting edge. A craft knife or hobby knife works well for projects using lighter-weight leather. Leather shears work well for cutting soft garment leathers but do not produce as accurate a cut as a sharp knife.

Rubber Cement and White Glue. These are used to prepare patterns. Either can be used, but rubber cement is easier to clean up.

Latex Gloves. These protect your hands while applying dyes and stains.

Cutting Surface. Use a hard rubber or polyethylene (or *poly*) board as a surface for all cutting and punching. The board will protect the work surface and will keep the edges of knives and punches sharp and undamaged.

Strap Cutter. Use to cut leather into straps of different widths for belts, dog collars, etc. Straps may be cut using a knife and ruler, but using a strap cutter is much easier, especially if you plan to make a lot of belts.

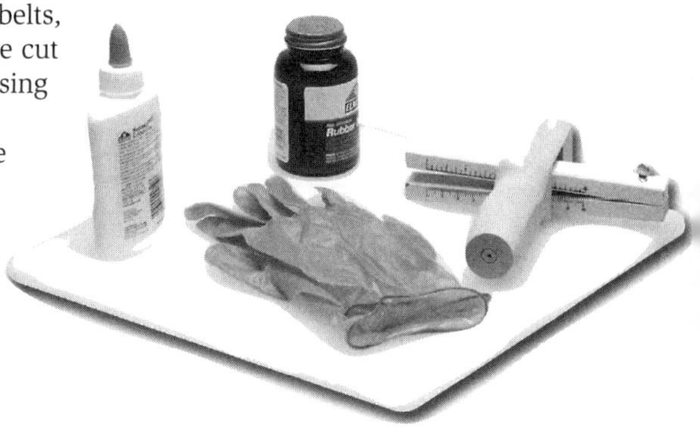

Tools for Decorating the Leather

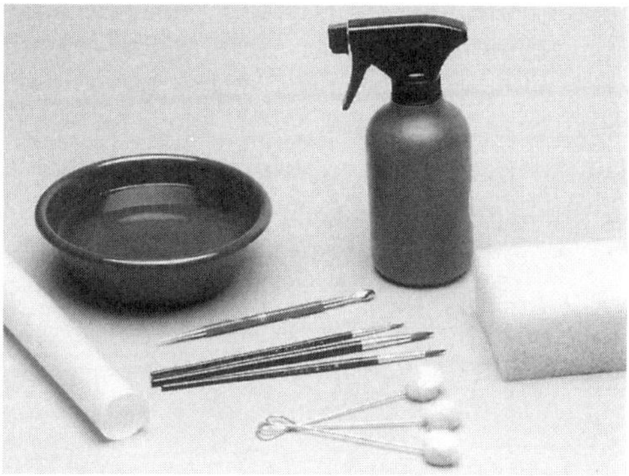

Tracing Film. A reusable plastic or polyester film that works like tracing paper. Use it to transfer sketched designs to leather. Tracing paper is not recommended because it is not as durable.

Modeling Tool. Use the pointed end of this tool to transfer designs from the tracing film to the leather. Use the spoon end, which comes in many shapes and sizes, to shape and smooth out the leather.

Applicators (Brushes, Wool Daubers). Use to apply dyes, stains, and finishes to leather projects.

Water Container, Sponge, and Spray Bottle. Use a plastic, glass, porcelain, or enameled container to hold water for dampening leather before it can be tooled, stamped, or molded. Never use a metal container for water. Water that is stored in a metal container will stain leather. Use a clean sponge to apply the water. A spray bottle also may be used.

Tooling Surface. A very hard, smooth surface is needed for tooling and stamping designs in leather. Marble is ideal, but granite, slate, countertop material, or pressed hardboard will work. A surface 1 to 2 inches thick and with a 6- to 12-by-12-inch surface will provide a good work area that is easy to move when not in use. A hard rubber cutting mat may be glued to one side of the stone to lessen the noise made while stamping and protect the top of the work surface.

Swivel Knife. Use to cut designs in leather. This knife gets it name because the yoke (finger rest), located on the opposite end from the blade, swivels. This swivel action makes it easy for leather-workers to control the movement of the blade as it cuts through the surface of the leather.

Metal-Stamping Tools. Use to make decorative impressions in leather. There are many stamping tools available, and each one produces a different impression. More complex designs may take any number of tools, but designs may be created using only one tool.

Mallet. Use for striking stamping tools, punches, and other tools used in leather-working. The mallet head *must* be made of rawhide, polyethylene *(poly)*, or wood, but never metal. Striking a metal tool with a metal hammer will damage a tool.

Edge Beveler. Used to bevel, trim, or round off edges of leather for a neater, more professional look. Available in several sizes; the smaller the number, the smaller the bevel. A size 2 is best for general leatherwork.

Tools for Adding Holes, Snaps, and Rivets

Hole Punches. Use to punch holes in leather for hardware and to punch holes for stitching and lacing. Two types of punches available are:

1. Single-drive punches, which punch a single hole when struck with a mallet. (Remember to use a rubber or poly cutting board under the leather when punching holes with a single-drive punch.)
2. Pliers-type punches, which punch a single hole when squeezed like a pair of pliers. Pliers-type punches are offered with a single-size tube (punch) or with up to six different sized tubes mounted on a rotating wheel.

Setters. Use for setting snaps and rivets in leather articles such as belts, pouches, sheaths, and other projects.

Make an ID Tag

A good first leatherworking project is an identification tag. As you move through the steps necessary to create the tag, you will learn many techniques used to make articles out of leather.

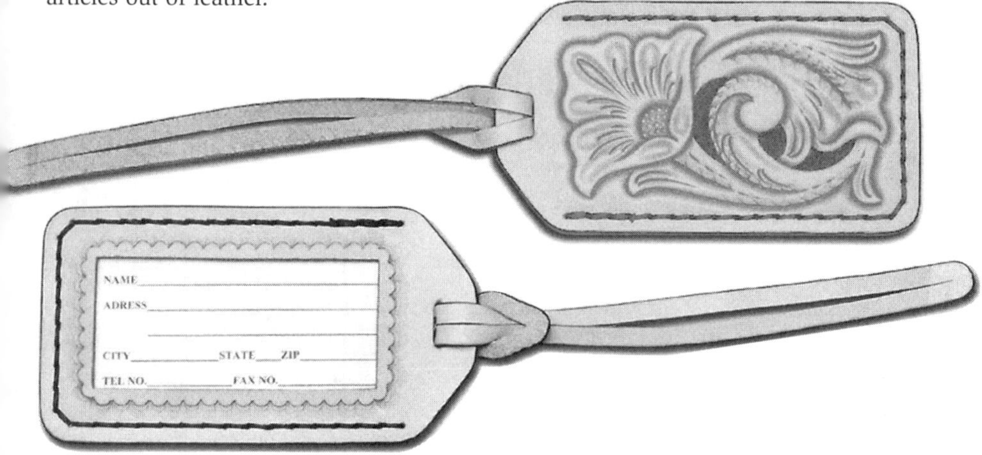

Pattern Layout and Transferring

To save time and leather, make a cutting pattern or template of the article you plan to make. This is simply a cardboard replica of the actual article, in this case, an ID tag.

Step 1—Begin by drawing on *paper* an article-sized pattern for each of the parts needed to make the tag. Mark the positions for all holes, slits, and the ID window cut-out.

Step 2—When you are satisfied that the patterns are correct, make a cardboard template of each part. To make the cardboard template, glue the paper pattern of each part onto cardboard with rubber cement or paper glue. (The cardboard back of a writing tablet works well for this.)

Step 3—Carefully cut out each part of the cardboard using the paper patterns as a guide.

Materials Needed

- ☐ General leatherworking tools and supplies (See the beginning of this chapter.)
- ☐ Scrap pieces of leather (for practice before using best leather)
- ☐ One 4- to 5-ounce piece of vegetable-tanned cowhide tooling leather
- ☐ One 2-inch-by-4-inch piece of clear plastic
- ☐ One 12-inch piece of waxed thread and stitching needle
- ☐ Choice of dyes or stains
- ☐ Leather finish

ID TAG CUTTING PATTERNS (ACTUAL SIZE)

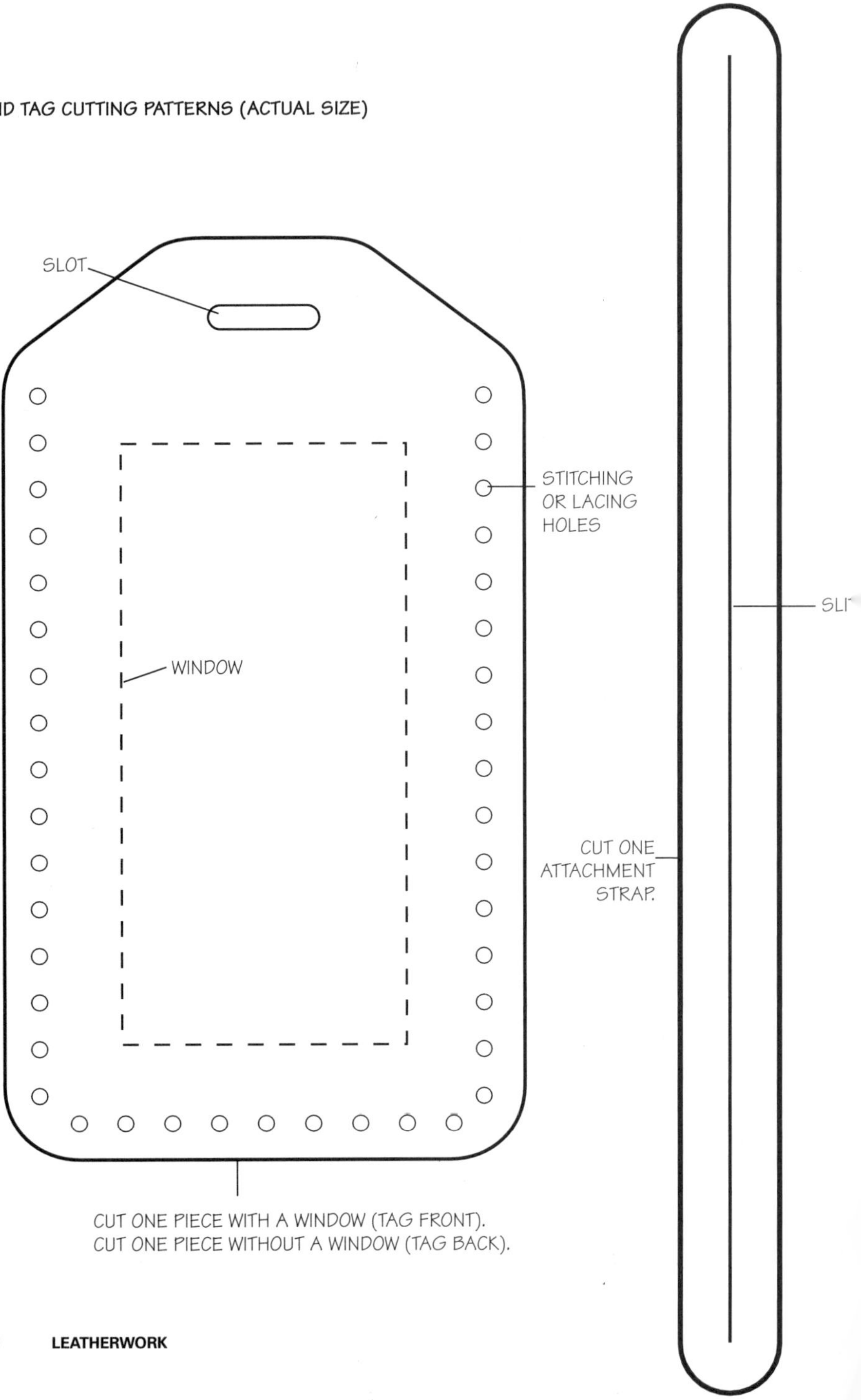

Cutting the Leather

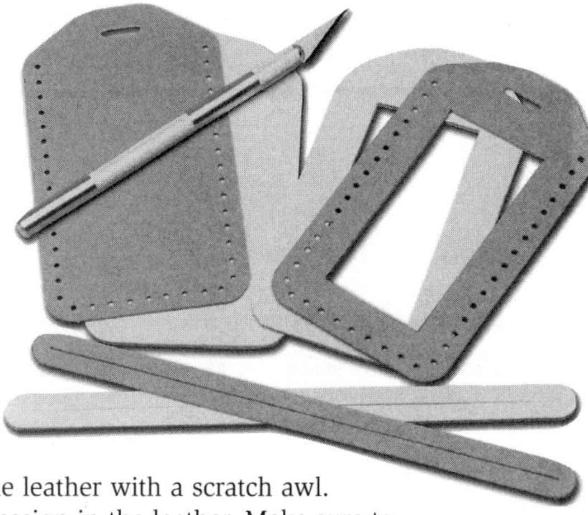

With the templates completed, you are now ready to cut the leather.

Step 1—Place the leather on the cutting surface with the fuzzy (flesh) side down. The smooth (grain) side of the leather should always be face-up for cutting.

Step 2—Position the templates on the leather so there will be little or no waste.

Step 3—Hold each template firmly and draw its outline into the leather with a scratch awl. The awl should leave a light impression in the leather. Make sure to mark all positions for holes, slot, slits, and the ID window.

Step 4—Carefully cut out each part with a leather knife. Try to cut through the leather with a single stroke; the cut edge of the leather will be cleaner and neater if you don't have to go over it again. Use a ruler as a guide for the knife on straight cuts.

Punching Holes

The next step after cutting out all the pieces is to punch holes to be used in stitching the project together, along with any slots or holes to be used for fasteners.

Step 1—Use a 1/16-inch hole punch to punch all stitching holes marked on the pattern. **Note:** The leather should always be dry when punching holes.

Step 2—To create the slot for the strap, use a 1/8-inch hole punch to make a hole in each end of the slot position. Then use a knife to cut out the leather in between the holes to create the slot.

Note: Remember to use a rubber or poly board under the leather when using drive punches. Hold the drive punch straight up and down and strike it firmly with a mallet, driving the punch through the leather.

Carved design

Stamped design

Decorating the Leather

Decorating leather by hand is one of the oldest and most fascinating arts known. The term *carving* refers to a design in leather that is first carved with a swivel knife, then various stamping tools are used to give the carved design a three-dimensional look.

The term *stamping* usually refers to a design in leather that is produced by using only stamping tools and a mallet.

PREPARING THE LEATHER

Before you can transfer, then carve, or stamp a design on leather, you must moisten the leather. A sharp swivel knife blade will cut easily and smoothly and stamping tools will imprint clearly and firmly into the leather *only* when the leather has been moistened (cased) to the proper degree. Knowing how moist a piece of leather needs to be to reach this degree comes with practice and personal preference.

Note: Always use glass, plastic, porcelain, or enameled containers for water. Never use metal containers. The slightest contact with metal will produce dark stains on leather.

Step 1—Wet the leather by *casing* it—simply rub a damp sponge on the flesh side of the leather as evenly as possible. Then turn the leather over and dampen the grain side (carving surface).

Step 2—When the dampened grain side of the leather has almost returned to its original color, it is ready to carve. Another test to know if leather is ready for carving is to hold the piece against your cheek. If it is dry, it will feel warm. If it is damp, it will feel cool. That is when the leather is ready to be carved. With practice, you will know instinctively when to begin carving.

Step 3—If some areas begin to dry, wipe the sponge over these areas to keep them damp enough to carve. If the leather is too dry, it will be too hard for you to cut with the swivel knife. If the leather is too wet, the cuts will not remain open.

If you must leave the dampened leather for an hour or longer, preserve its moisture content by putting it into a plastic food bag. If any drying spots have appeared, apply moisture lightly with a sponge before storage. To prevent mildew from forming, store the covered leather in the refrigerator until you are ready to work again.

Transferring the Design

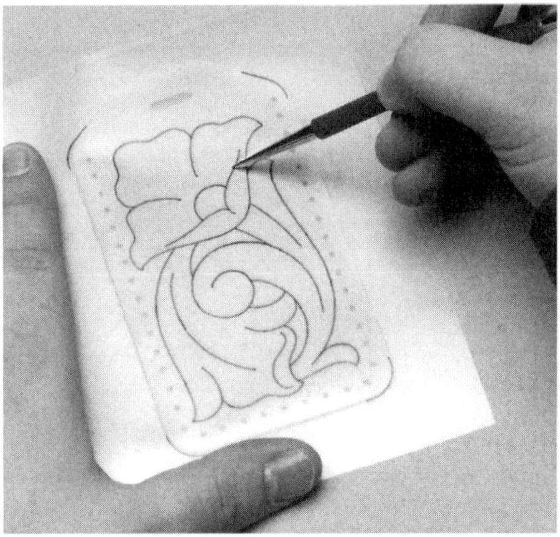

Step 1—Whether you choose to carve or stamp the leather, it is easier if you first draw the main outlines of the design onto tracing film.

Step 2—When the surface of the dampened leather begins to return to its original color, it is time to transfer the design to the leather.

Step 3—Place the tracing film in position on the leather. Carefully trace over the lines with a stylus. Use no more pressure than you would for writing with a pencil on paper. The pressure of the stylus pressing on the tracing film will leave an impression of the line on the leather. Before removing the film, lift up one corner to make sure all the lines of the design have been transferred.

SAMPLE TRACING PATTERN FOR BACK OF THE ID TAG (ACTUAL SIZE)

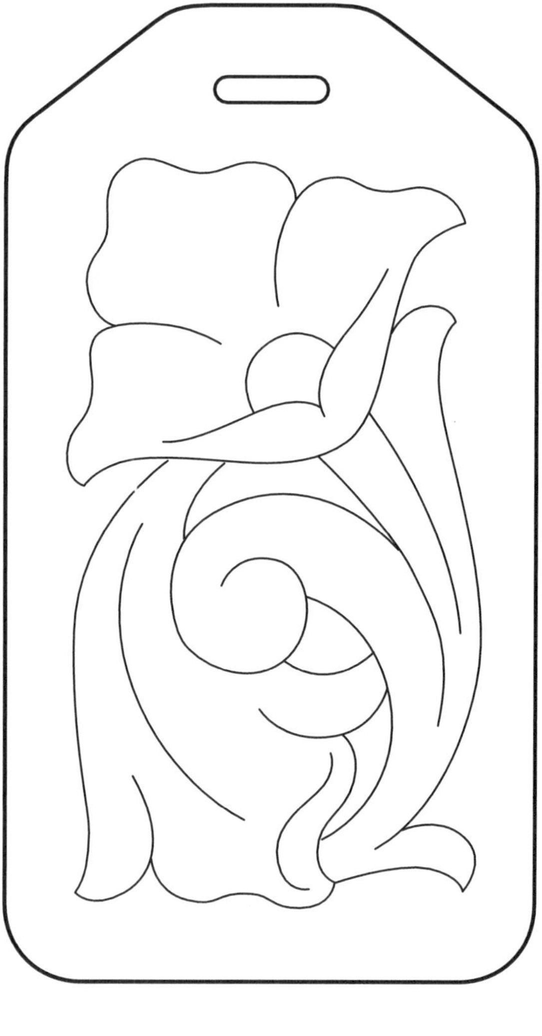

Carving the Leather

It's now time to bring the design to life by carving and stamping with various tools. To help ensure success, read this chapter carefully, follow the instructions, and practice on pieces of scrap leather.

SWIVEL KNIFE

The most important tool used in carving leather is the swivel knife. It is used to cut the main outline of the design and put decorative cuts in the finished piece. Study thc illustrations shown here and practice making some cuts on scrap leather before starting on the project.

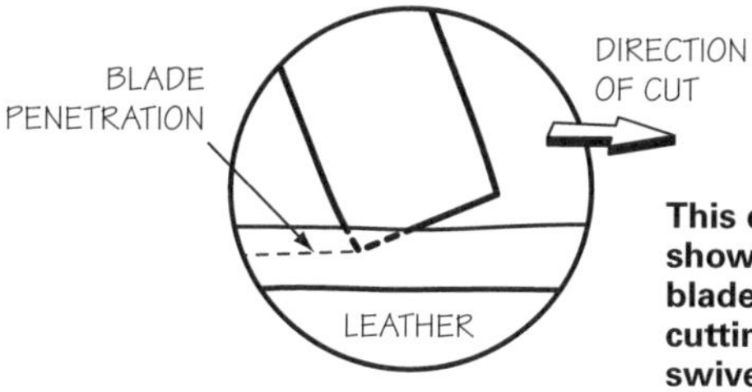

This cross-section shows the proper blade angle for cutting with the swivel knife.

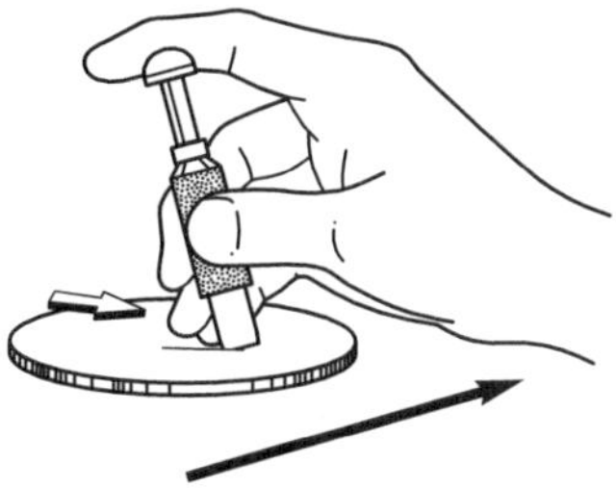

Keep the side of your hand on the work surface to steady the cut.

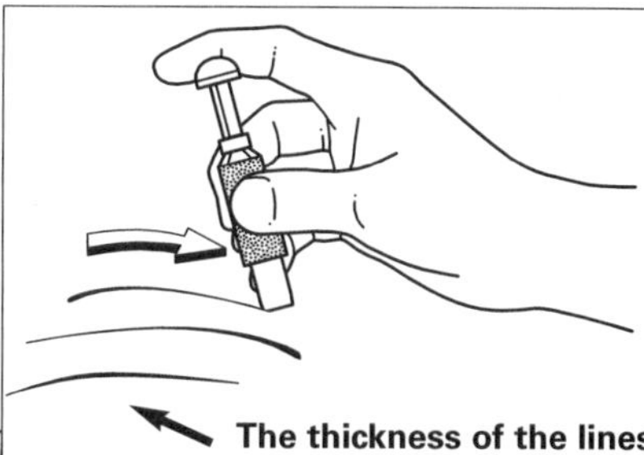

The thickness of the lines in the illustration shown here indicates the point of the most pressure applied to the blade.

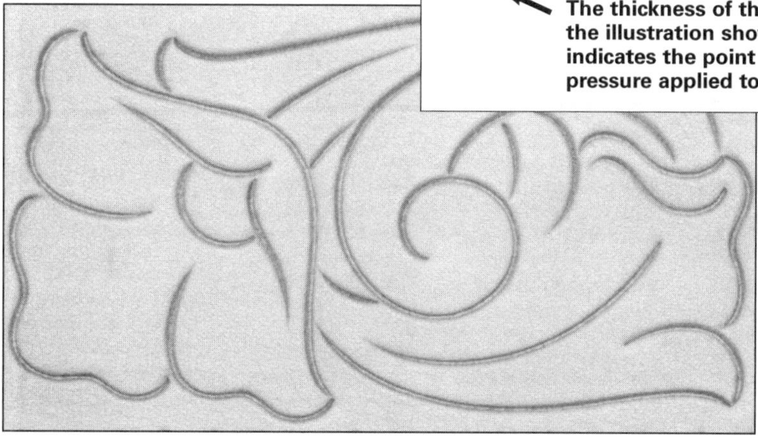

CAMOUFLAGE

The camouflage is used next. It is designed to add texture to certain parts of the design. Practice first holding the camouflage tool straight up and down, striking it sharply with the mallet. Try leaning it to one side or the other to vary the impressions. Study the illustration to learn the proper use of camouflage.

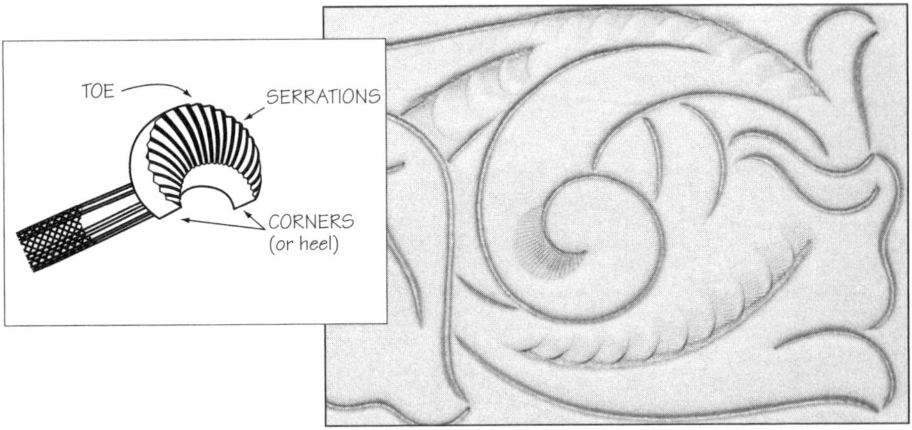

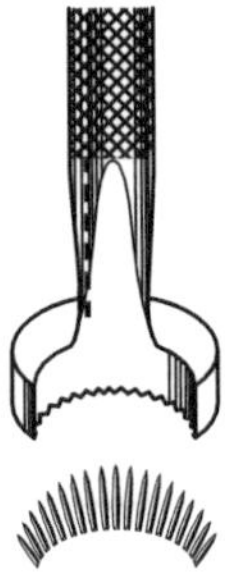

FULL IMPRESSION
This is a full impression of the stamp. Hold the tool straight up and down, then strike it sharply with the mallet so that all the lines are equal in depth.

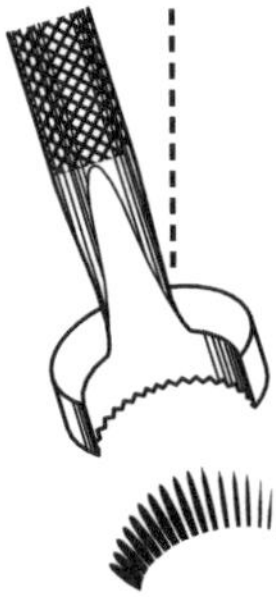

LEFT-CORNER IMPRESSION
Lean the tool to the left. Hold the tool securely so that it does not slip when struck with the mallet. Impressions on the right side should appear to fade to nothing.

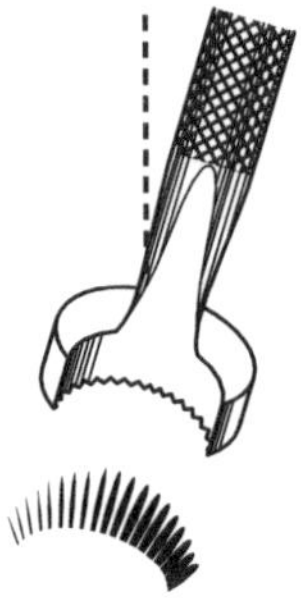

RIGHT-CORNER IMPRESSION
Leaning the tool to the right fades the left-corner impressions and firmly imprints the right corner of the tool. Hold the tool firmly to keep it from slipping.

TOE IMPRESSION
Here the tool is tipped forward on the toe so that the corners do not dig in. The tool usually is tapped lightly in this position.

PEAR SHADER

The pear shader is used to shape the areas outlined by the swivel knife. It creates low spots and high spots for a more natural look to the design. Hold it straight up and down, and practice "walking" the pear shader. Think of it as a jackhammer, and use short, even strokes as you move the tool just slightly as you go. Study the photo to learn what areas are shaded by this pear-shaped tool.

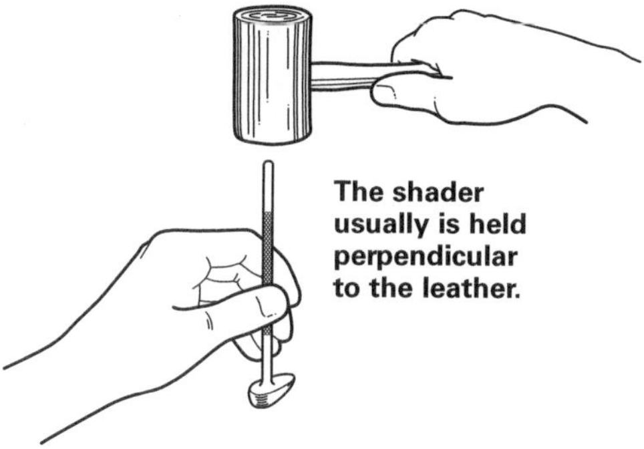

The shader usually is held perpendicular to the leather.

Lessen the force of blows as the area to be shaded diminishes.

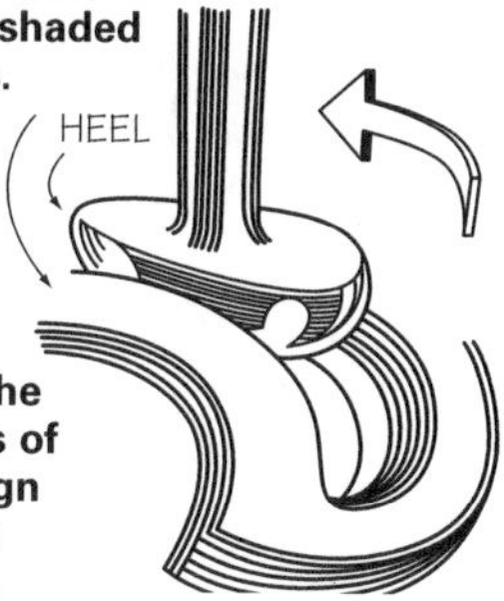

Follow the contours of the design with the shading.

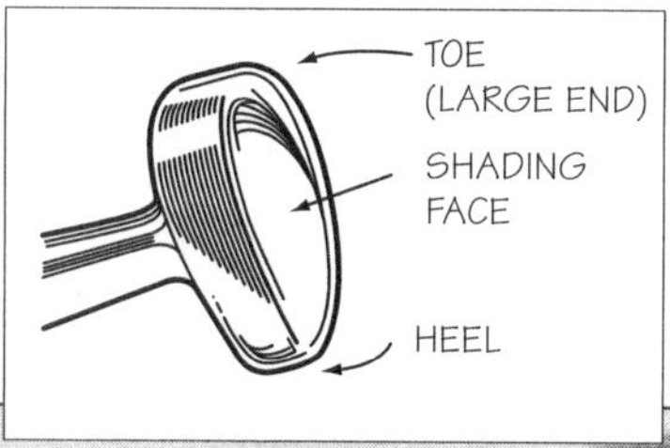

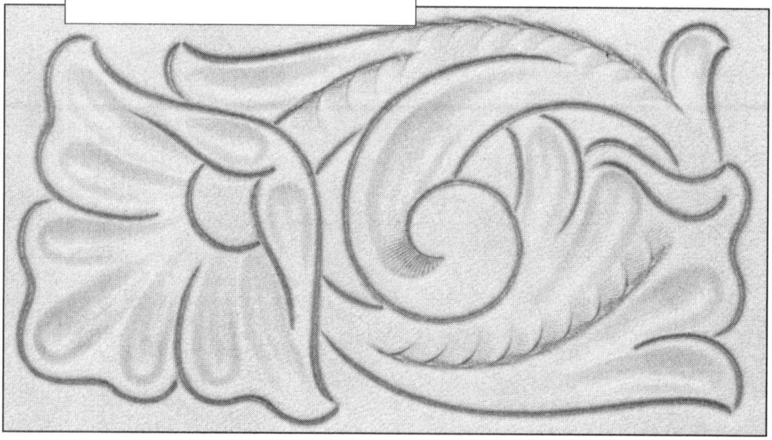

BEVELER

The beveler is another "walking" tool, used to lower the areas around the design so that the design appears raised. Areas within the design are also beveled to create an overlapping effect from one part of the design to another. The toe of the beveler follows the lines made by the swivel knife. Study the photo to see how proper beveling brings the design into bold relief. Practice on scrap leather to get the feel of "walking" the beveler.

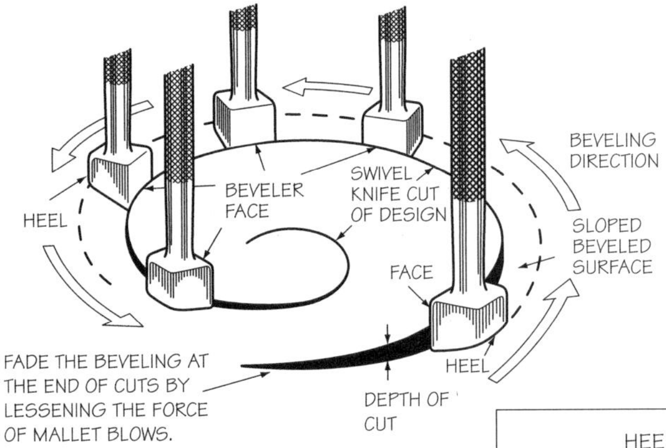

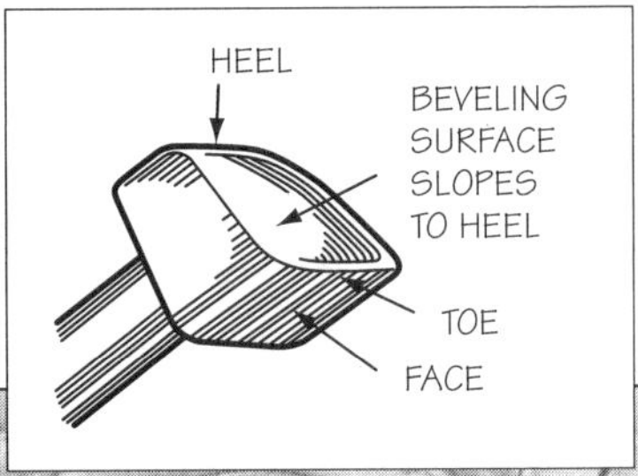

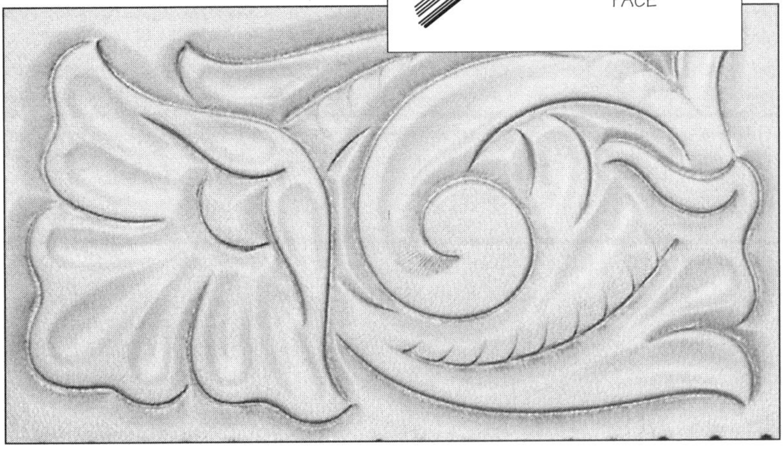

VEINER

The veiner is used to add veins to leaves and for other special effects. Like the camouflage, the veiner is often leaned to one side or the other. The angle of the tool determines the length of the impression and makes it fade out as it goes away from the swivel cut. Study the illustrations to see how this tool is used.

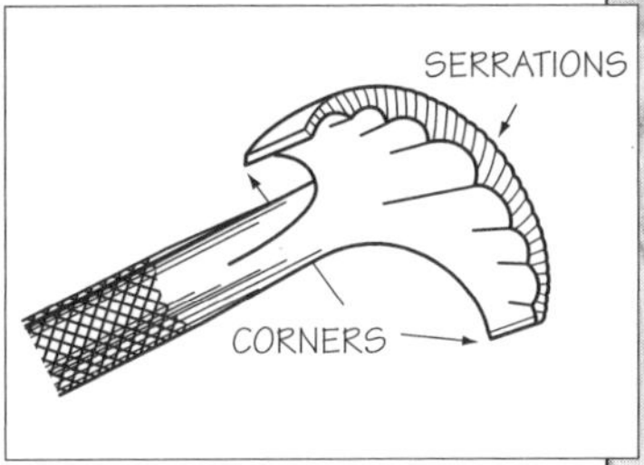

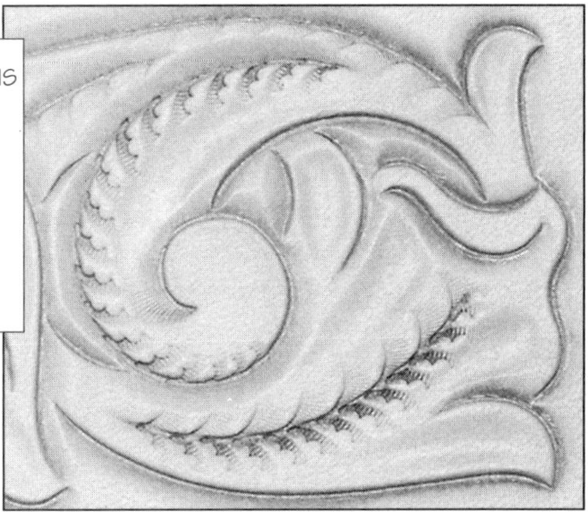

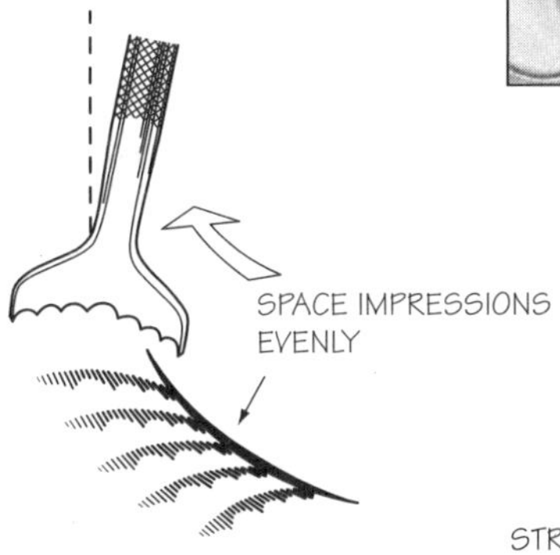

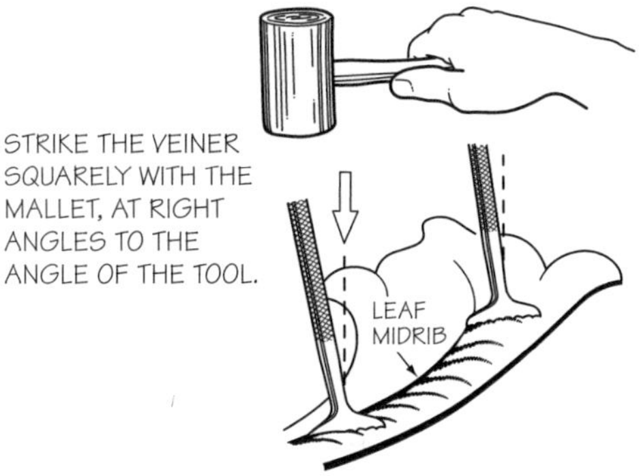

SEEDER

The seeder is used for making seed pods in the flower center. This tool is much smaller than the others, and it doesn't take nearly as much force to make a deep impression in the leather. The outer row of seeds is stamped first, then the second row, and so on until the pod area is filled.

Begin stamping the outer row of seeds first. Stay within the cut line, and space the impressions as close together as a string of beads. Near the end of a row, adjust the spacing so that the last seed does not overlap the flower petal.

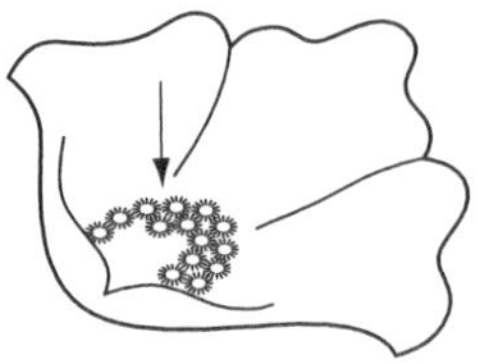

Stamp the second row of seeds, stacking them close to the first row and keeping them as even as possible. Do not overlap.

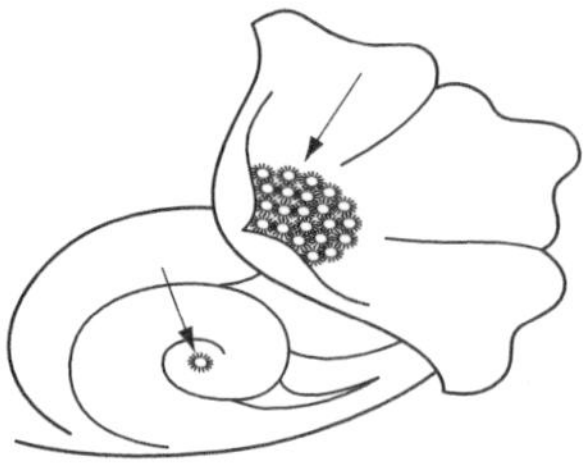

Fill in the remaining area. Stamp seeds carefully. Only the serrated edges should touch or overlap. Optional: Place a seed in the center of the scroll.

BACKGROUNDER

The backgrounder pushes down the background within and around the design to make it stand out. Hold the tool straight up and down and try to make each impression the same depth. Rotate the tool with your fingers as you go to avoid creating a tool pattern. Notice in the photo how even the background area looks—you can't tell the shape of the tool that was used to make these impressions.

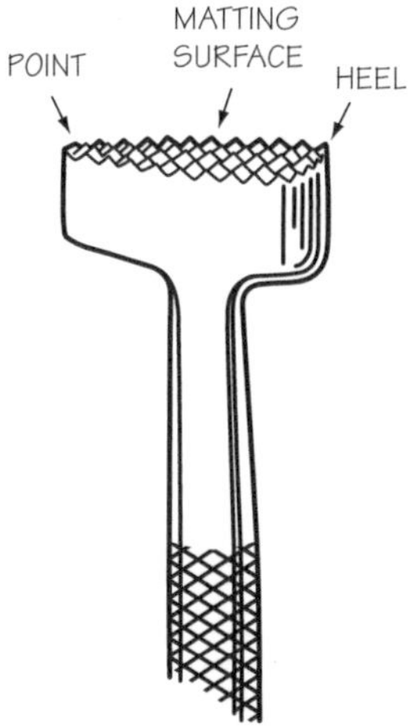

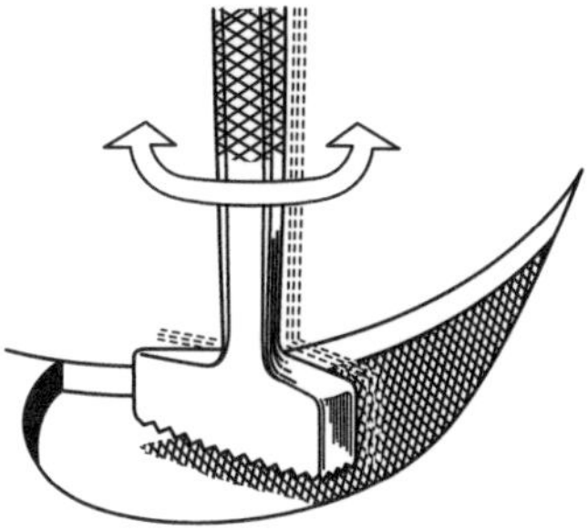

Hold the background tool straight up and down.

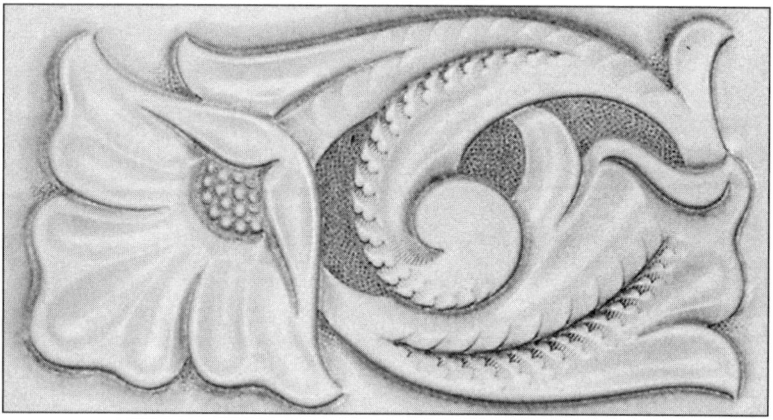

DECORATIVE CUTS

The photo here shows the completed tooling with the addition of decorative cuts. These are done with the swivel knife and should always flow in the direction of the design. It takes lots of practice to do these well. So, practice, practice, practice! It's best to practice on pieces of scrap leather before applying decorative cuts to your actual project.

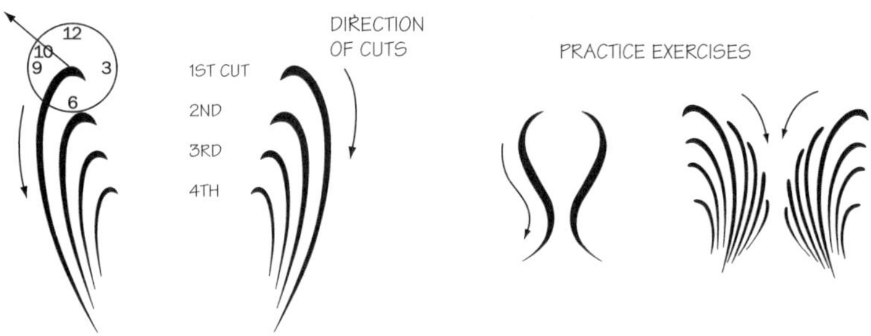

When adding decorative cuts, make the long cuts first. Practice rights and lefts, first for motion and flow to get the feel of decorative cutting. Then, practice control to make the cuts successively shorter and to make them gracefully graduate toward each other at the ends of each cut.

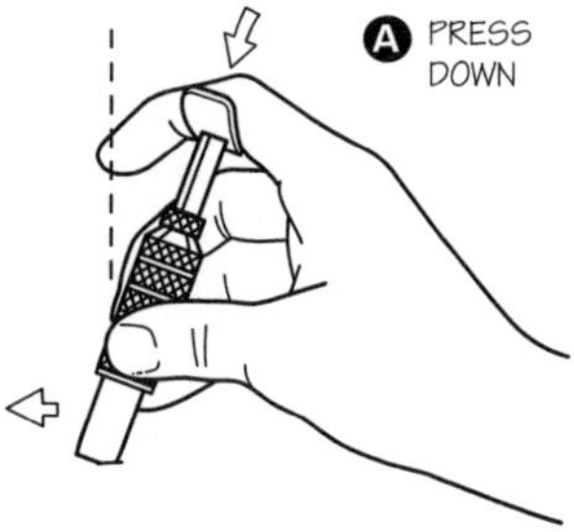

For a right cut, your hand must be rolled to the right to bring the blade into proper cutting position. Begin with heavy downward pressure to make the cut pop open. The blade should be pointed at 10 o'clock as illustrated.

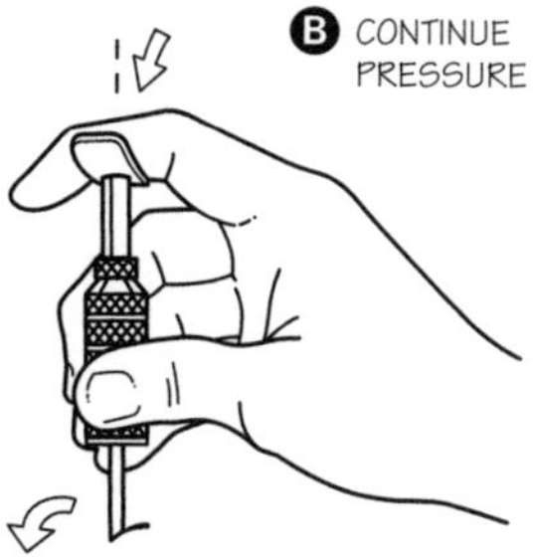

Begin the turn immediately, straightening your hand to almost normal position as the blade turns toward your body. Continue heavy downward pressure.

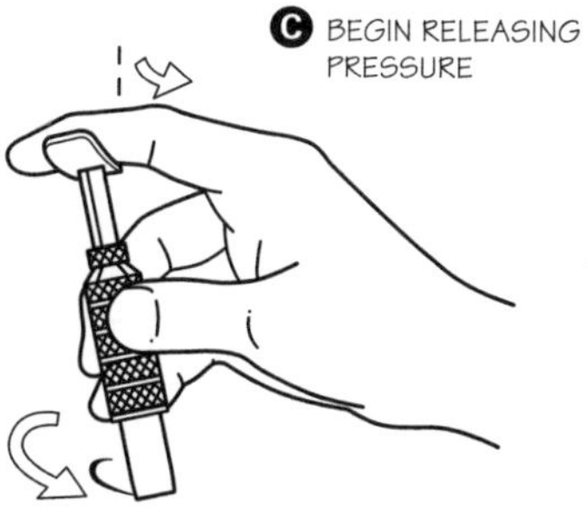

As the cut begins to straighten, pull your hand and arm toward you to steady and control the cut. Gradually diminish the pressure on the yoke.

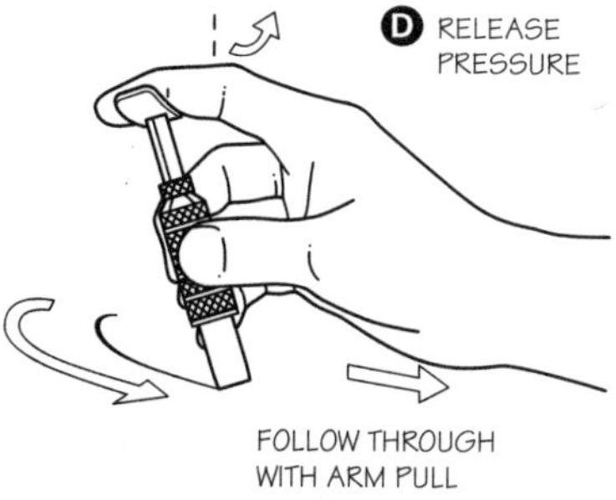

Continue the cut in one graceful, flowing movement, simultaneously lessening the depth of the cut with each motion of progress. Fade the cut to a hairline and continue the follow-through motion as you lift the blade from the leather.

Stamping the Leather

Many beautiful designs can be created without the use of a swivel knife.

ADD A BORDER

A single camouflage stamping tool can be used to add an attractive border. To do this:

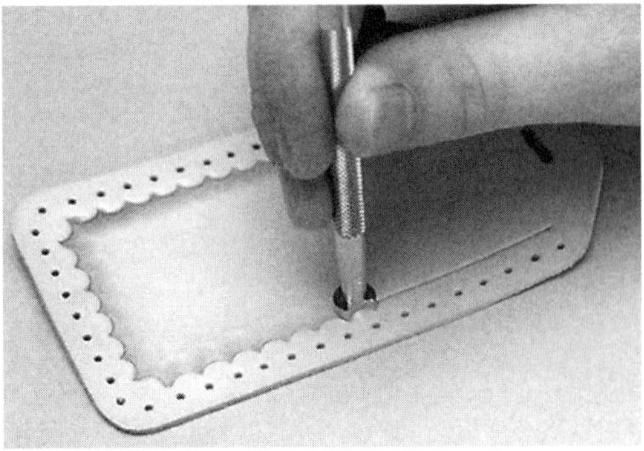

Step 1—Draw a guideline into the dampened ID tag leather with the pointed end of a modeling tool or wing divider. Make this guideline approximately 3/8" in from the edges, as shown here.

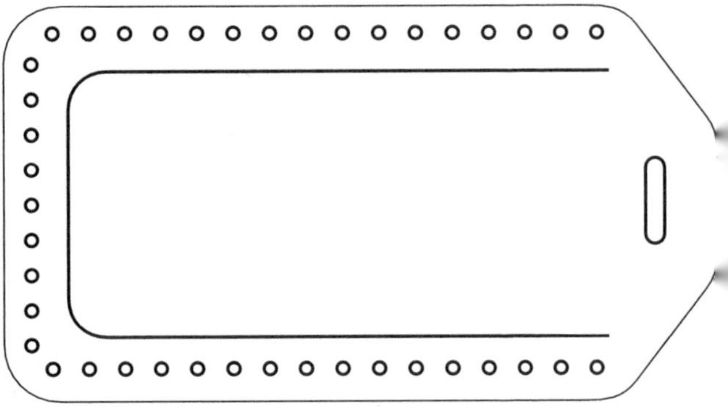

Step 2—Set the camouflage tool on the guideline. Hold the tool straight up and down, then strike it firmly with a mallet. Move the tool over to the next position and strike again. Repeat this all the way around the tag. Adjust the distance between the impressions so the corners will work out evenly.

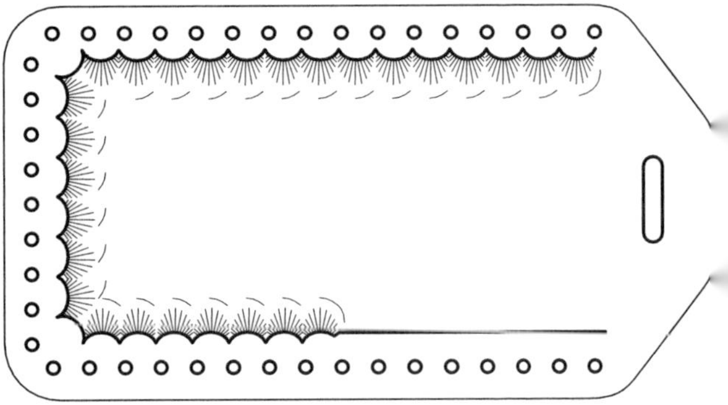

The samples here show a few of the many designs you can create using stamping tools. But don't limit yourself to the designs shown here. Experiment! You will be surprised at the many designs you can create using different combinations of stamping tools.

Articles made from leather may be personalized by adding names or initials. Use a swivel knife and beveler or special alphabet stamps.

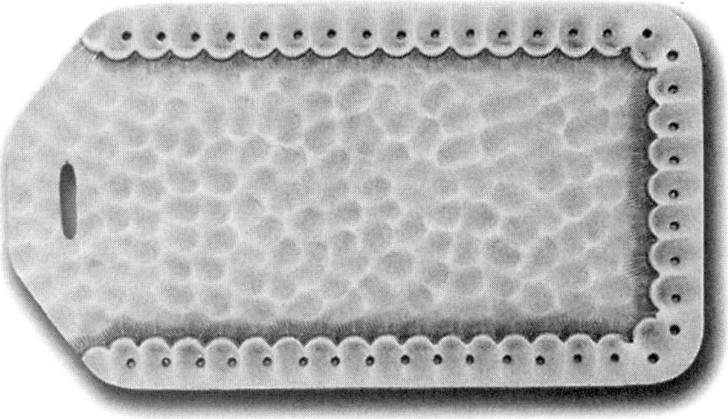

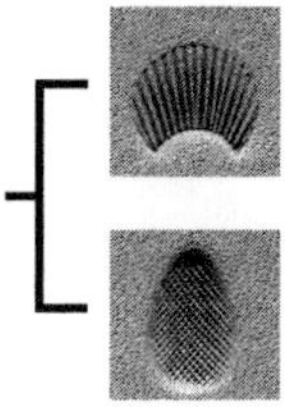

Two stamps used to create design

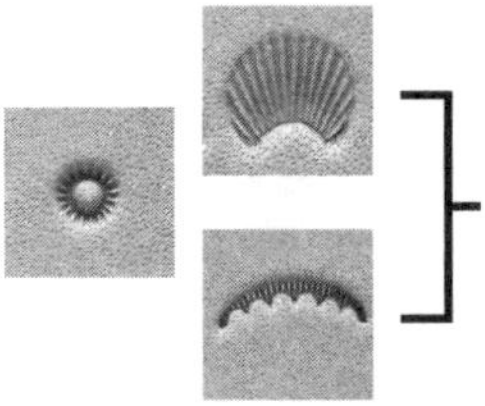

Three stamps used to create design

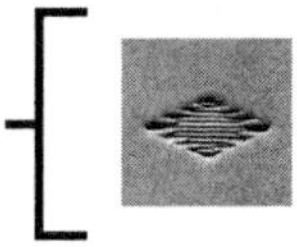

One stamp used to create design

Dyes, Stains, and Finishes

Leather projects may be left in their beautiful natural state with only a clear finish added for protection. You may want to enhance the design or change the natural color of the leather by adding dye or stains.

Spirit dyes should be applied with brushes for small areas and with wool daubers for larger areas.

APPLYING SPIRIT DYES

Spirit dyes usually have an alcohol base, which requires extra safety precautions during use. Never leave spirit dyes within reach of children. Always close the cap between applications to prevent spills. Protect hands from direct contact with oil and spirit dyes, as stains are difficult to remove from the skin.

Before using dyes, stains, or finishes, protect the work surface by covering it with brown paper. Wear latex gloves to protect hands from direct contact with oil and spirit solvent dyes, as stains are difficult to remove from skin.

To apply a dye in a solid color:

Step 1—Dip the applicator in the dye and begin in the upper left-hand corner. Move quickly in a circular motion so that each stroke lightly overlaps the last, as shown.

Step 2—When the strokes of color begin to thin, dip the applicator into the dye and resume the overlapping circular motion until the entire project has been covered.

Step 3—One application of dye usually is not enough. Apply a second "coat" of dye over the entire project *in the opposite direction,* repeating steps 1 and 2.

Repeat steps 1 through 3 as needed to achieve the results you want.

Background Dyeing With Spirit Dyes. Spirit dyes can be used for coloring the background of leather projects. Use a No. 3 sable brush, and leathercraft dye thinner to clean the brush. First, practice on scrap leather. "Twist" the brush clockwise to point the bristles, an important technique when applying spirit dyes.

Dip your brush in the dye. Always touch the brush to a piece of scrap leather first to remove excess dye. Too much dye will *bleed* over the edges of the design. Begin by applying the dye in an open area, toward the center of the background. This will help prevent bleeding, as well. Use short, pulling strokes.

When most of the dye on the brush has been exhausted, twist the brush clockwise *on a piece of scrap leather,* and complete the dyeing using an outward stroke in an open area.

In difficult areas, turn the leather as often as necessary to help facilitate the dyeing.

DYEING THE BACKGROUND WITH SPIRIT DYES

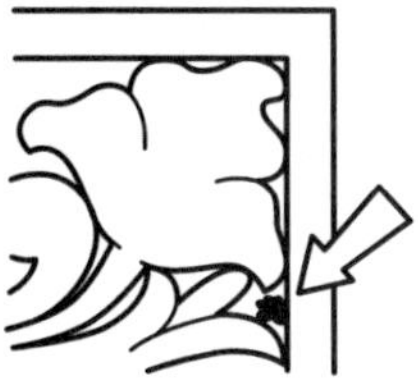

Correct method: Here the brush was pushed to the center of the background first, minimizing the danger of dye bleeding over the design.

Incorrect method: Here dyeing was started in a small area. Excess dye has spread and crawled over the edges of the design.

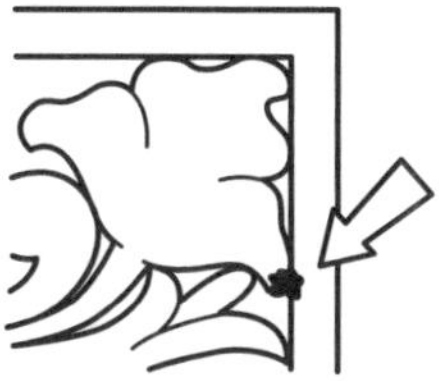

APPLYING ANTIQUE STAINS

The purpose of antique staining is to achieve a rustic, antique color tone while letting the grain of the leather show through. Antique stains are thicker than spirit dyes and should be applied heavily over the entire piece.

Step 1—Using a damp sponge, apply a liberal coat of antique stain, rubbing in a circular motion until the color is even and all cuts and stamped impressions are filled.

Step 2—Allow the stain to dry 5 to 10 minutes or until set. **Note:** Do not allow antique stains to dry more than 15 minutes.

Step 3—Using a clean, damp sponge, remove the excess stain from the surface of the leather, until the desired contrast is achieved.

Step 4—After the stain dries, buff the surface of the project with a soft, clean cloth.

Step 5—To protect the antiqued surface of the project, apply a finish.

The difference between a dye and a stain is that a dye generally is used to completely cover portions of a project with color, while a stain is used to create highlights on the entire stamped or tooled project.

APPLYING FINISHES

Natural leather requires a finish to protect it from water and dirt and to give it an attractive shine. Some finishes are water-based, others are lacquer. Your choice will depend partly on what type of dye, if any, you used on the leather. Ask a leather-craft dealer for advice on this area, or follow the directions on the dye bottle.

Before applying the finish, there are several points that you should know:

- All tooling of the design must be complete before finish is applied.
- The surface area must be clean, dry, and free of any dirt, dust, or other matter.
- Leather finish must be applied prior to assembly. It is difficult to get a smooth, even coat over a curved structural surface.

To apply a leather finish, follow these steps:

Step 1—Press a sponge dampened slightly with water to the top of a bottle of leather finish, and tip the bottle so a little finish flows onto the sponge.

Step 2—Apply a light coat of finish to the carved side of the leather, moving the sponge in a circular motion over the leather. Work the finish into the cuts and impressions.

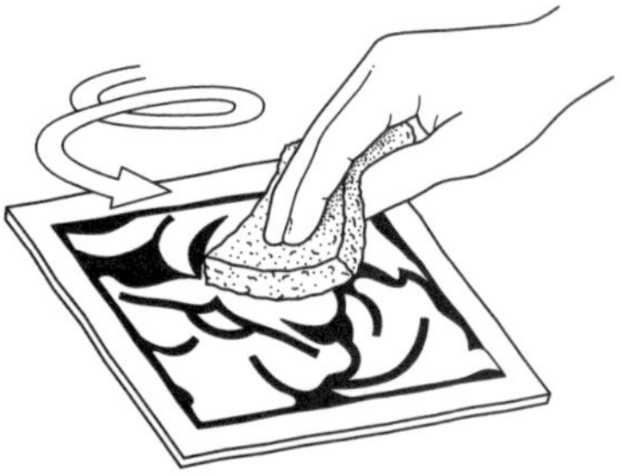

Step 3—Let the finish dry thoroughly, then apply a second coat if you desire a shinier finish. Allow the piece to dry thoroughly.

Step 4—If a high gloss is desired, buff the leather with a piece of woolskin or a clean, soft, lint-free cloth.

The project is now ready to be assembled, either by stitching with waxed thread or by lacing with leather or plastic lace.

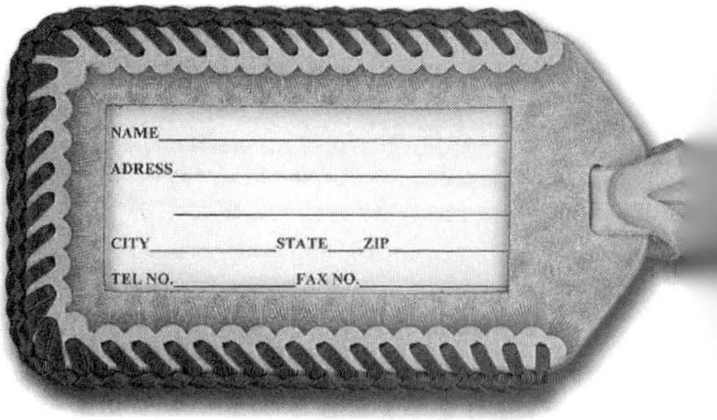

Lacing makes this ID tag much more attractive. A hand-stitched tag appears at the beginning of this project.

Assembly by Lacing or Stitching

There are many ways to lace together a project and many different materials that can be used for a variety of effects.

Lacing. The most popular lace is 3/32-inch calf lace. It is easy to work with, extremely durable, and attractive. Lacing techniques include the whip stitch, running stitch, and double-loop lacing.

Hand-stitching. Many leathercrafters prefer to assemble their projects with waxed thread. Techniques include single- and double-needle hand-stitching.

To prepare the project for lacing or stitching, follow these steps:

Step 1—Cement the flesh (rough) side of the front pieces to the flesh side of the back piece, lining up the edges and holes. Be careful not to cement the top, unpunched area of the pieces so the ID card can be inserted and removed.

Step 2—Insert a 2-by-4-inch piece of plastic and an ID card into the tag so the information on the card shows through the window in the front.

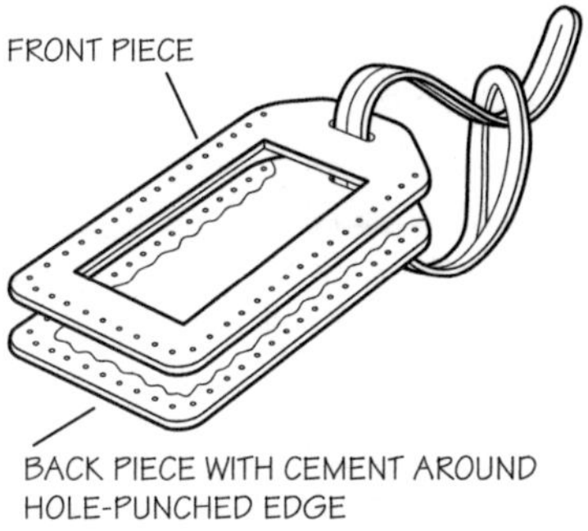

Align the front and back pieces prior to lacing or stitching.

Step 3—Push one end of the strap through the slots in the ID tag, then thread the end through the slit in the strap and pull snug to secure.

Step 4—Attach the tag to the handle of suitcase, duffel bag, or backpack by looping the loose end of the strap around the handle. Then push the tag through the slit in the strap and pull snug to secure.

Step-by-Step Assembly Techniques

THREADING A TWO-PRONG NEEDLE

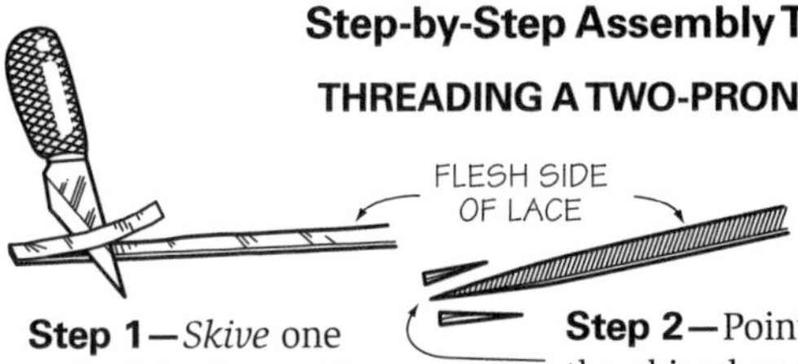

Step 1—*Skive* one end of the lace with a sharp knife.

Step 2—Point the skived end of the lace.

Step 3—Spring open the threading end of the needle.

Step 4—Insert the pointed end of the lace into the needle.

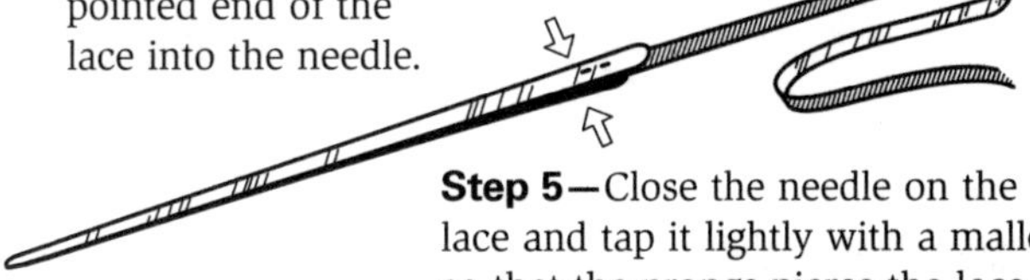

Step 5—Close the needle on the lace and tap it lightly with a mallet so that the prongs pierce the lace and lock in place.

WHIP STITCH

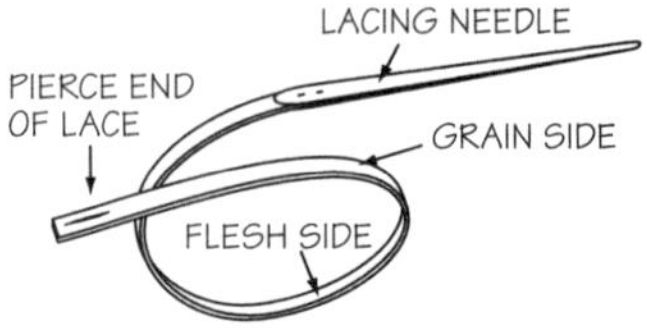

Step 1—Thread the needle; pierce the opposite end of the lace with a sharp knife, leaving a 1/8-inch slit.

Step 2—Start between the two layers of leather. Leave 1/4 inch at the end where you slit the lace.

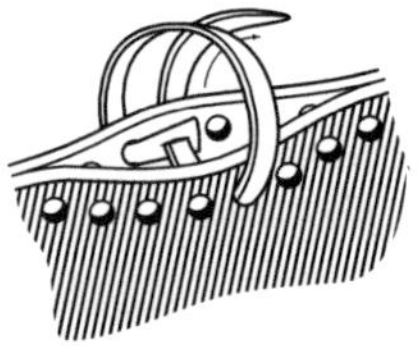

Step 3—Push the needle through the second hole, then the slit, then the opposite hole.

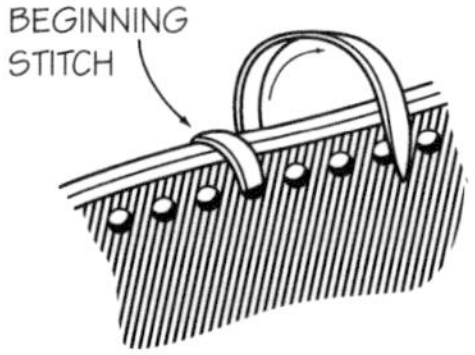

Step 4—Pull the stitch up tight. Continue lacing, tightening the lace as you go.

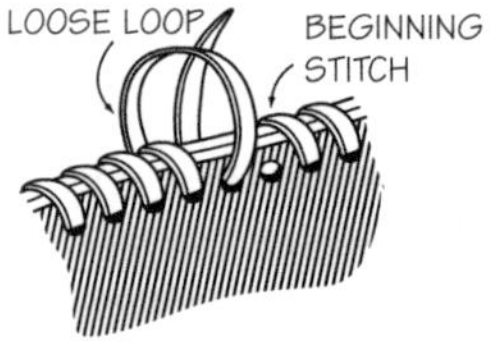

Step 5—Lace around the project, leaving a loop in the second hole from the beginning hole.

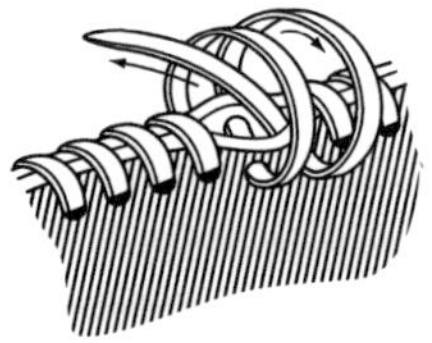

Step 6—Lace through the last hole, up between the leathers and through the first loop.

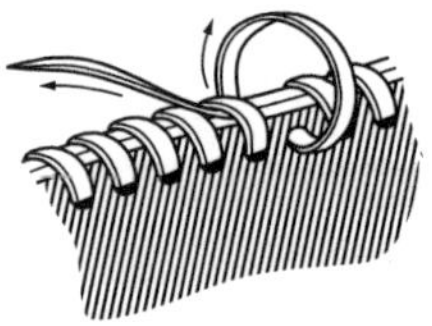

Step 7—Pull the first loop tight, over the end of the lace.

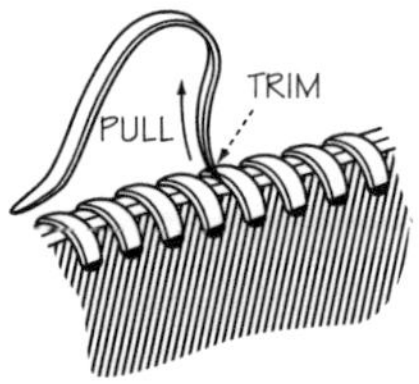

Step 8—Pull the end of the lace tight to take the slack out of the last loop. Trim off the end of the lace and tap all lacing flat with a mallet.

RUNNING STITCH

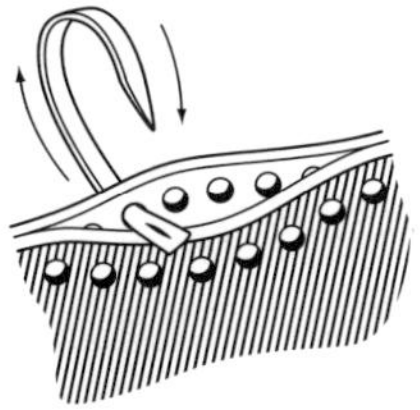

Step 1—Begin lacing as for step 2 of the whip stitch.

Step 2—Push the needle through the next hole from the back, through the slit, and out through the opposite hole in front.

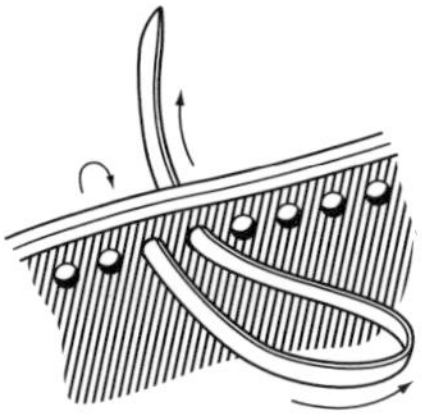

Step 3—Pull the stitch up tight to lock the lace. Continue lacing the rest of the project.

Step 4—Pull the beginning stitch up tight and continue lacing, pulling the stitches tight as you go.

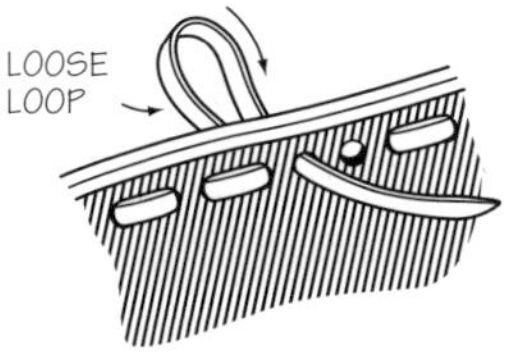

Step 5—Lace to the last hole and leave a loose loop in the second to the last hole.

Step 6—Push the needle through the last hole. Spread the leathers; push the needle through the next-to-last hole, bringing the needle up between the leathers.

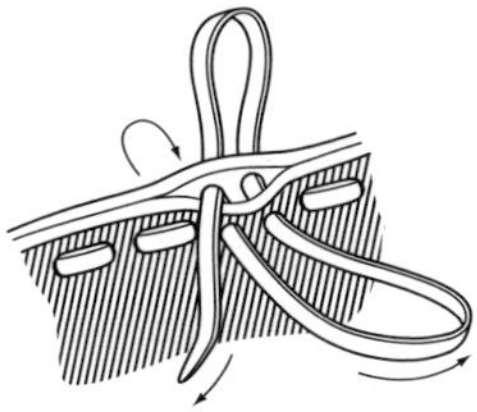

Step 7—Pull the loose loop tight and continue pulling all the slack out of the lace.

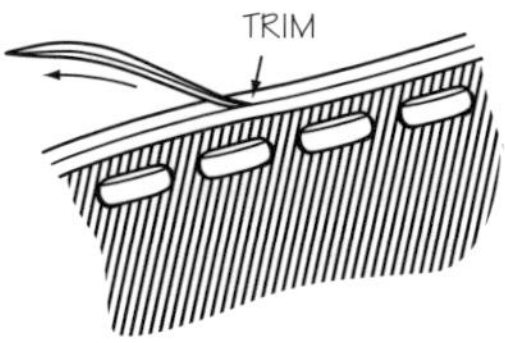

Step 8—Pull all the stitching up tight; pull the end of the lace tight. Trim off the end of the lace close to the leather and tap all lacing flat with a smooth mallet.

DOUBLE-LOOP LACING

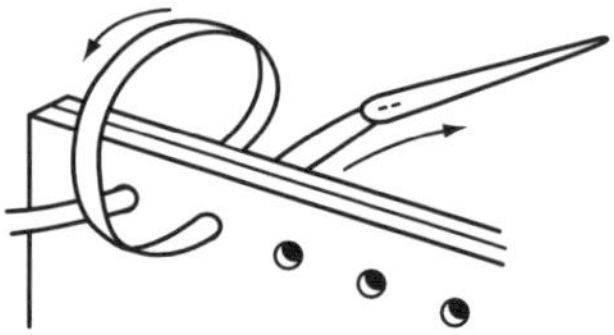

Step 1—Beginning on the front side of the project, pull the needle and lace through the first hole. Leave about 1/4 inch of the lacing end and go on to lace the next hole.

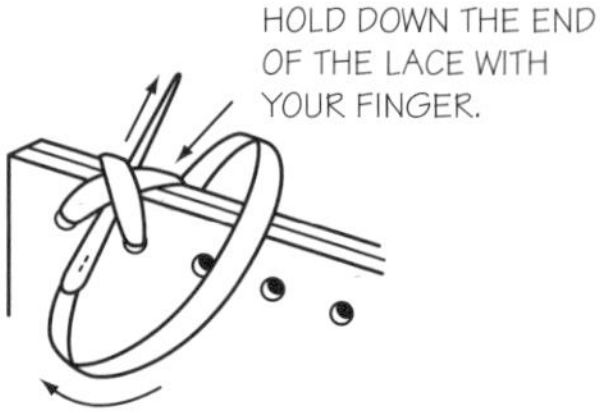

Step 2—Pull the stitch tight, lacing over the end you left free. This forms a cross or "bight."

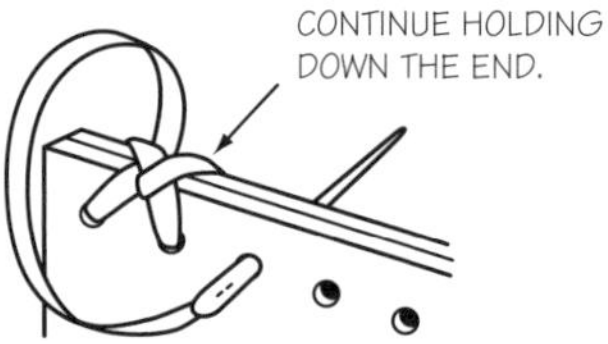

Step 3—Pull the stitch under the bight. Pull it snug, but not tight. Lace through the next hole.

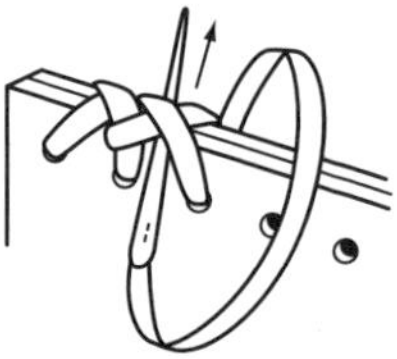

Step 4—Follow the same procedure as in steps 1 and 2, making a cross or bight. Once again stitch under the bight (step 3) and pull the stitch snug.

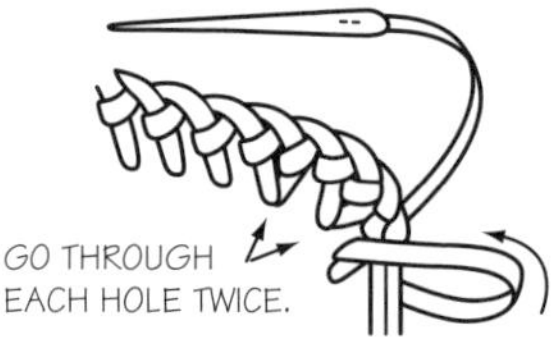

Step 5—When lacing a corner, stitch through the three corner holes (twice each). Be sure to go through a bight on corner stitches.

Tip: Avoid twisting the lace as you pull it through the holes.

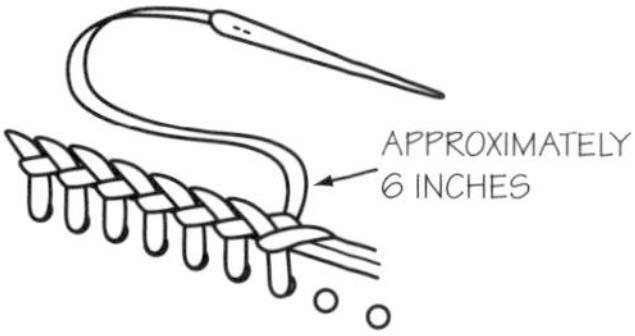

Step 6—Lace until only 5 or 6 inches of lace remains. You will have to splice with a new length of lace.

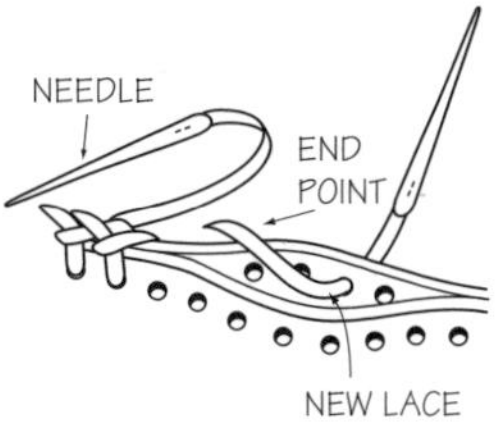

Step 7—Insert the new lace down between the leathers, four holes from the first lacing. Pull out the back side. Leave 3/4 inch of lace between the leathers.

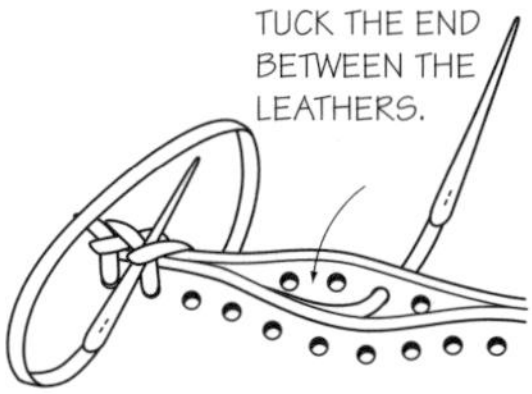

Step 8—Tuck the end of the lace between the leathers and continue lacing the project with the first lace.

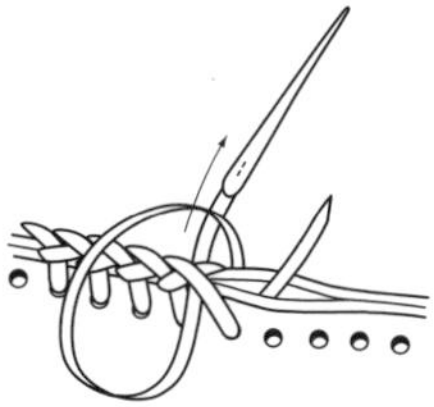

Step 9—Pull the first lace up tight. Trim the end at an angle, allowing about 3/4 inch to remain.

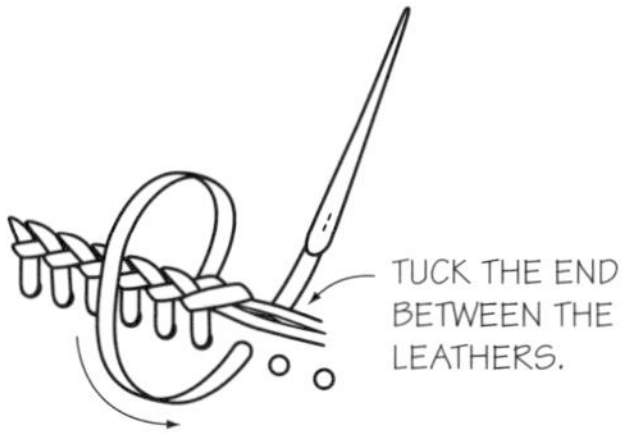

Step 10—Tuck the end of the first lace between the leathers and lace over it with the new lace so that it is caught and won't show.

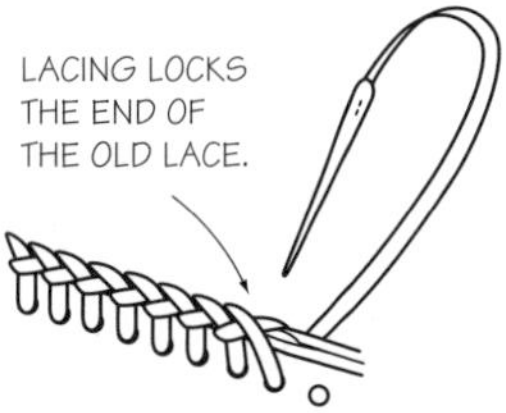

Step 11—Continue lacing to the starting point.

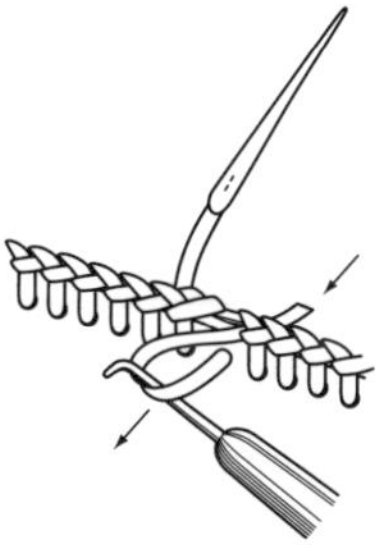

Step 12—Tie off the lacing by pulling the end of the beginning lace free of stitches.

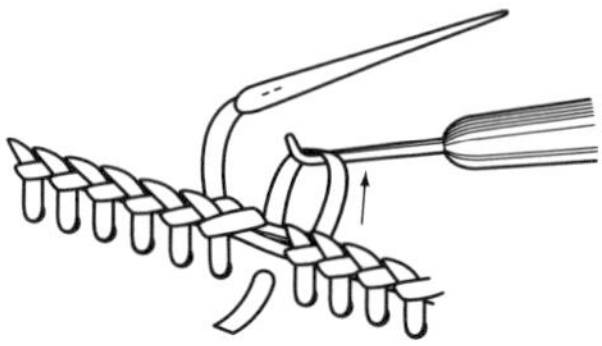

Step 13—From the back side, pull the end of the lace out of the hole.

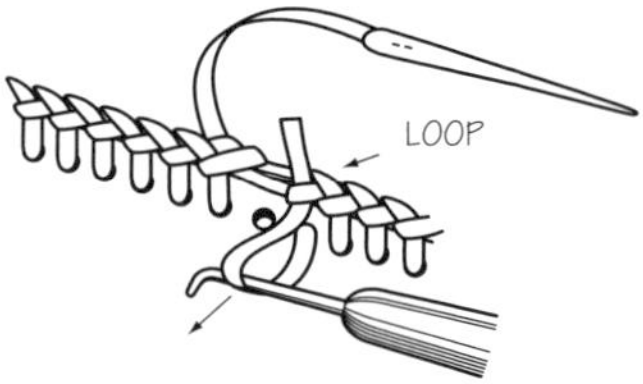

Step 14—From the front side, pull the end of the lace out of the loop.

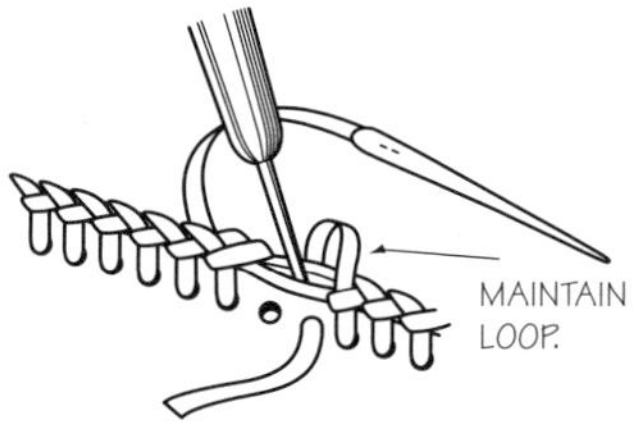

Step 15—Push the needle down between the leathers and hook it over the lace.

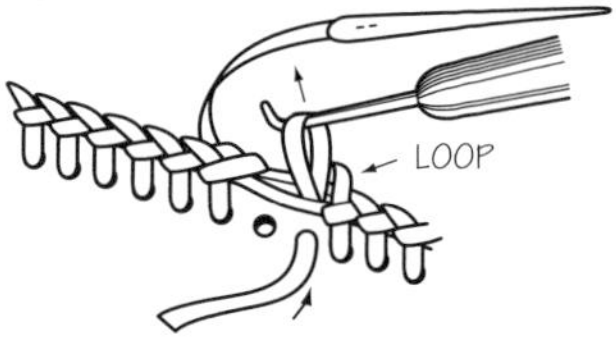

Step 16—Pull the end of the lace out of the hole and up between leathers. Two empty holes should appear on the front side and one on the back.

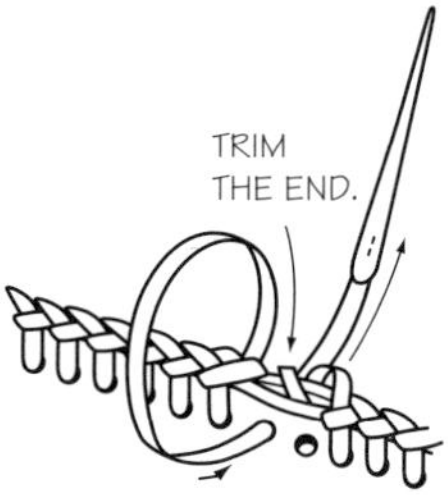

Step 17—Trim the end of the lace you have pulled out and tuck the end of the lace between the leathers. Lace through the next hole.

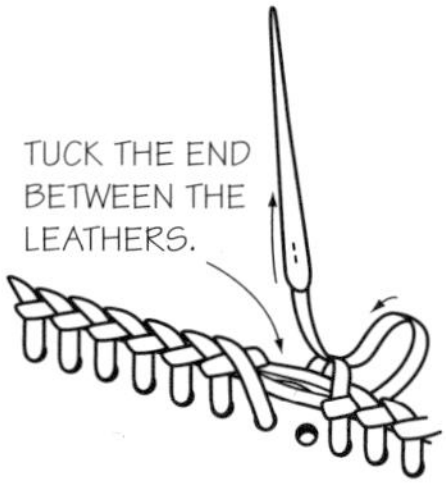

Step 18—Pull the stitch tight and lace up through the loop from the back side. All holes on the back side should be filled.

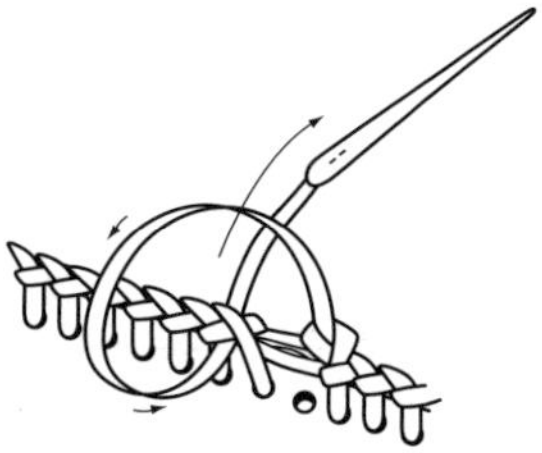

Step 19—Lace under the bight. Do not pull this stitch tight.

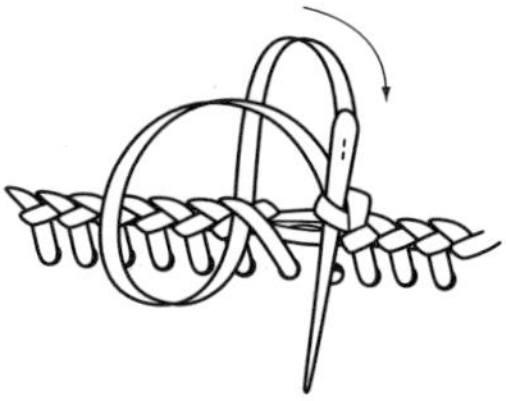

Step 20—Carefully cross over as shown and push the needle down through the loop.

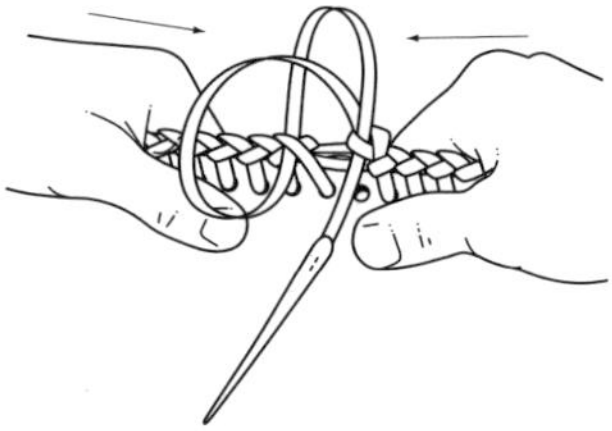

Step 21—Pull the needle through. Push the laced edges together to adjust the starting loops for easier completion.

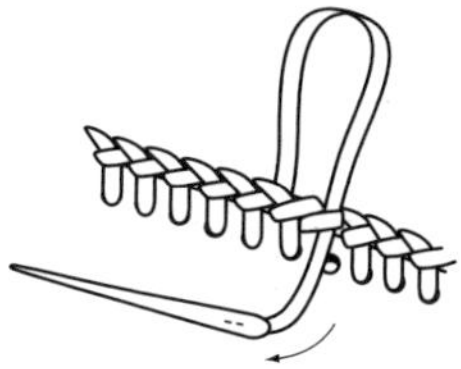

Step 22—Pull any slack out of the first loop and adjust the lacing with your fingers to make all the stitches appear equal.

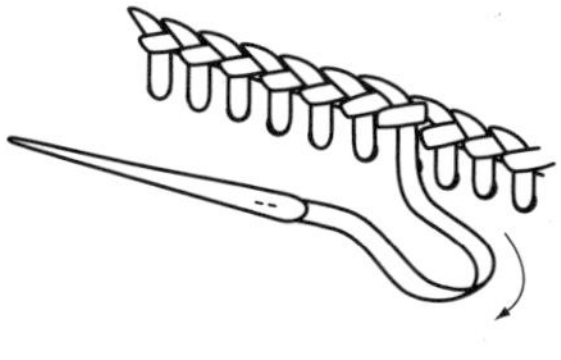

Step 23—Pull the end of the lacing down tight. Make sure all stitches appear even and equally spaced.

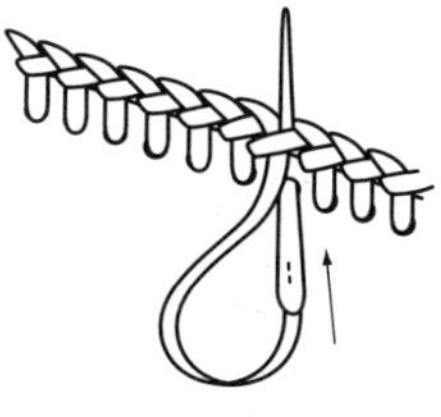

Step 24—Push the needle through the last hole as shown. Bring it up between the leathers and out between the lacing. Trim the excess lace.

SINGLE-NEEDLE HAND-STITCHING

Step 1—Thread one end of waxed thread through the eye of the needle and pull about 1 inch through. Wrap the end around the thread and twist it between your fingers. Push the needle through first hole in the top piece only, leaving a 1-inch tail of thread between pieces of leather. Stitch down through the second hole in both pieces of leather and up through the third hole. Continue stitching in this manner to the last hole, pulling each stitch tight.

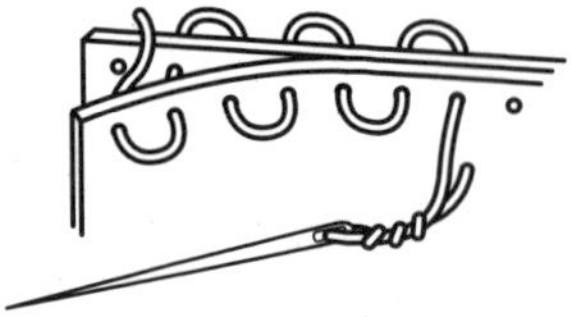

Step 2A—When you reach the last hole, turn and begin stitching back to the starting point, filling in alternate stitches. Stitch to the beginning hole.

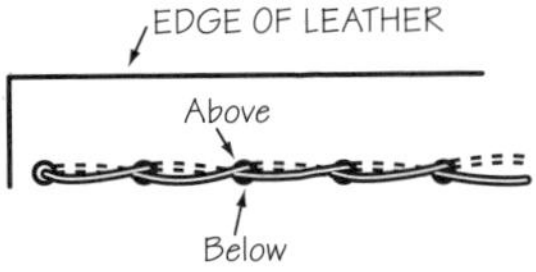

Step 2B—Optional, for a more professional look when filling in the stitches: From one side, put the needle through the hole above the previously stitched thread. From the other side, put the needle through the hole below the previously stitched thread and pull each stitch tight. Continue stitching in this manner.

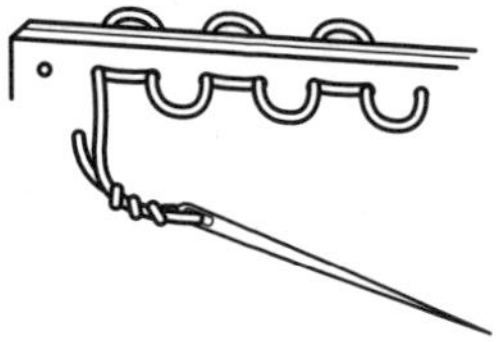

Step 3A—When you reach the beginning hole, go through the hole in the bottom piece only and bring the needle up between the two pieces of leather. Trim the excess thread. Tap down the stitches with a mallet.

Step 3B—Alternate ending: When you reach the beginning hole, go through the hole in both pieces of leather and then stitch back through the next three holes and pull each stitch tight. Trim the excess thread close to the leather on the outside, and tap down the stitches with a mallet.

DOUBLE-NEEDLE HAND-STITCHING

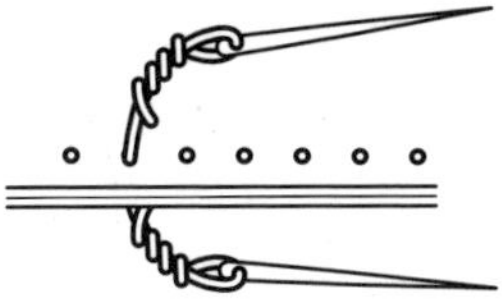

Step 1—Thread one end of waxed thread and pull 1 inch through. Wrap the end around the thread and twist it between your fingers. Place a needle on the other end of the thread in the same way. Push one needle through one set of aligned holes on the side of project and pull it through until the same count of thread is on each side.

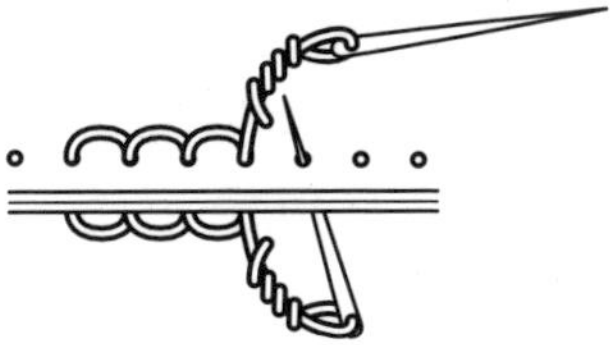

Step 2—Holding the project between your knees, push the needle on the inside through the next hole and pull through. Push the outside needle through the same hole, being sure to go over the first thread. Grasp both threads and pull the stitch tight. Continue stitching this way all around the project, pulling each stitch tight.

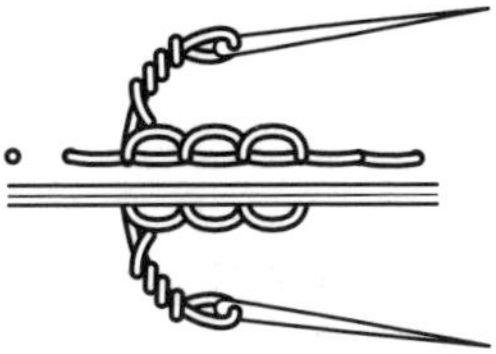

Step 3—When you reach the last hole, stitch back through the preceding three holes, pulling each stitch tight. Trim the excess thread close to the leather on the outside and tap down the stitches with a mallet.

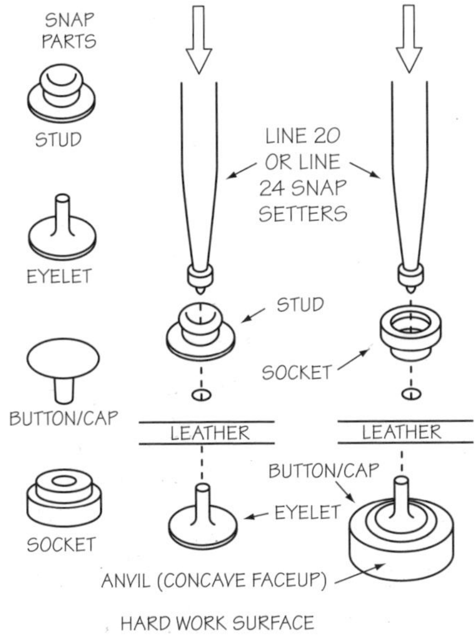

Setting Snaps and Rivets

The article you construct out of leather might need snaps or rivets. These are normally used for attaching buckles, closing flaps, or reinforcing stress points. The instructions shown here tell what tools are necessary and how to use them to set the most common types of snaps and rivets.

Setting line 20 or 24 snaps

Setting rivets

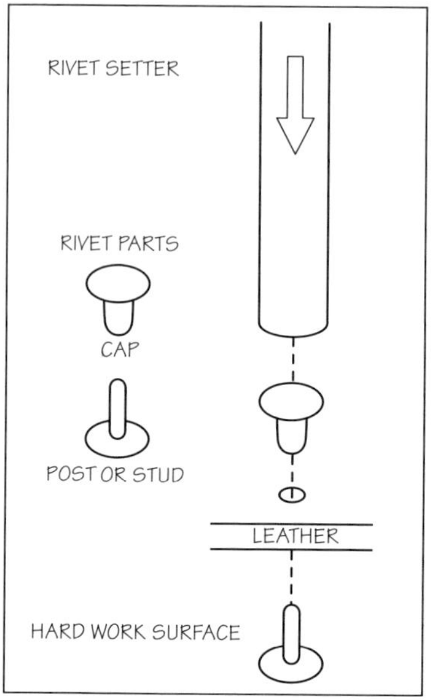

Use whichever setting instruction fits the needs of the project. Strike the appropriate setter firmly with a rawhide, poly, or wooden mallet until the fastener, snap, or rivet is set.

Never strike setting tools with a metal-face hammer. Doing so will damage the setting tools.

Setting glove or belt snaps

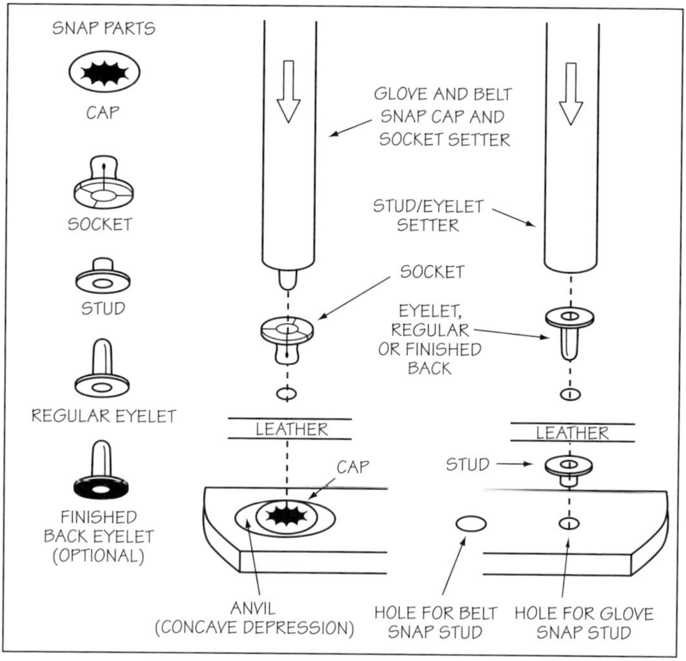

Dressing the Project

You can improve the look and feel of projects by dressing or finishing the edges.

Step 1—Bevel or round off the edges of the project with an edge beveler. A size 2 edge beveler works the best on projects made out of 4- to 9-ounce (4/64-inch to 9/64-inch) leather, including belts.

Step 2—Once you have rounded the edges of the project with an edge beveler, use a sponge to slightly dampen the edges with water.

Step 3—*Burnish* or slick all rounded edges by rubbing the edges back and forth briskly with a folded piece of canvas or coarse cloth. A properly dressed edge should have a darkened, polished look.

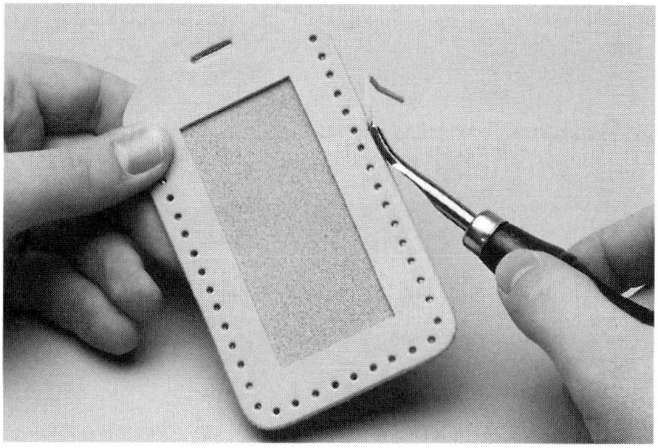

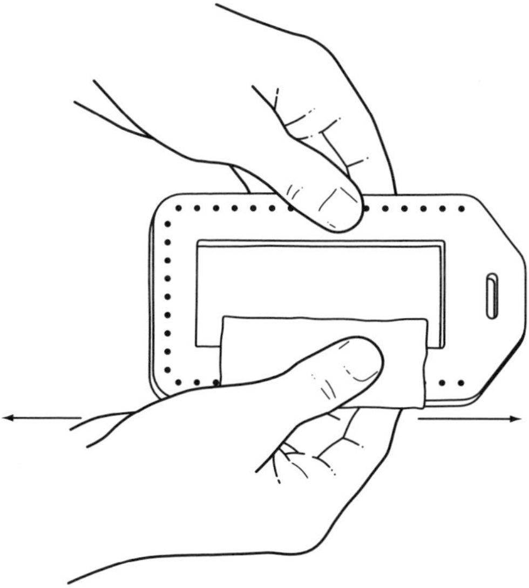

Make a Belt

The belt project will use the following techniques:

- Sizing
- Cutting
- Punching holes and slots
- Dressing edges
- Setting snaps

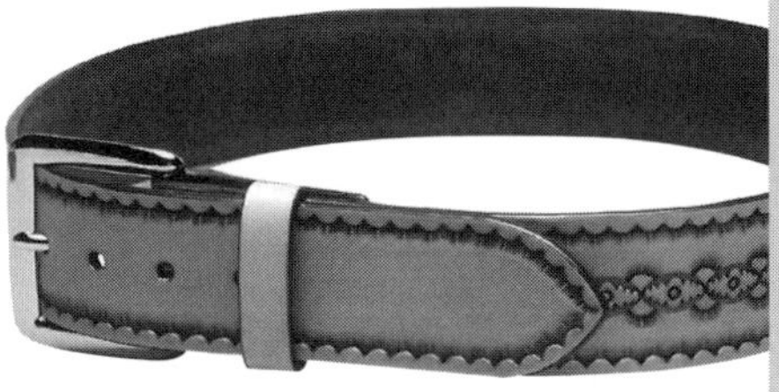

Materials Needed

- ☐ General leatherworking tools and supplies (See the beginning of this chapter.)
- ☐ One 7- to 9-ounce vegetable-tanned cowhide tooling leather belt strip (The width can vary, although $1\frac{1}{2}$ inches is the most popular.)
- ☐ One buckle to match the intended width of the belt
- ☐ Two belt snaps
- ☐ No. 2 edge beveler
- ☐ One 7-inch-by-$\frac{3}{4}$-inch piece of leather for a belt keeper (optional)
- ☐ Tools for stamping and/or carving a name or designs
- ☐ Choice of dyes or stains
- ☐ Leather finish

Determining Waist Size

The first step in making a belt is to determine the waist size. Use one of two methods.

Method 1. Pull a measuring tape snugly over pants around waist, outside the belt loops. Do not pull the tape too tight.

Method 2. Lay an old belt on a work surface as straight as possible. Measure from the end of the buckle tongue to the hole most used.

Getting Started

Step 1—Cut or buy a strip of leather of the desired width that is 8 to 10 inches longer than the waist size. On the back side, measure back $2\frac{1}{2}$ inches from the buckle end and mark a fold line on the leather.

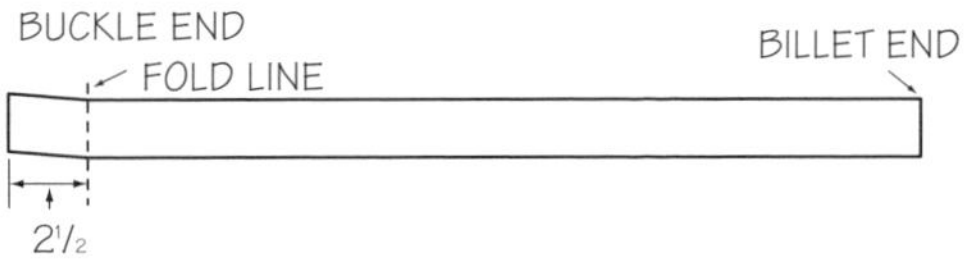

Step 2—Place the buckle with the bar at the fold line. Begin from the tip of the buckle tongue and measure the waist line. Mark the end of the waist size. This will be the center hole of the billet end.

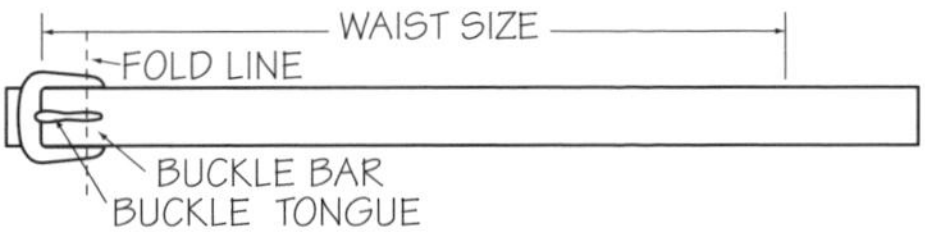

Step 3—Mark, then punch, a slot for the buckle tongue and holes for the belt snaps.

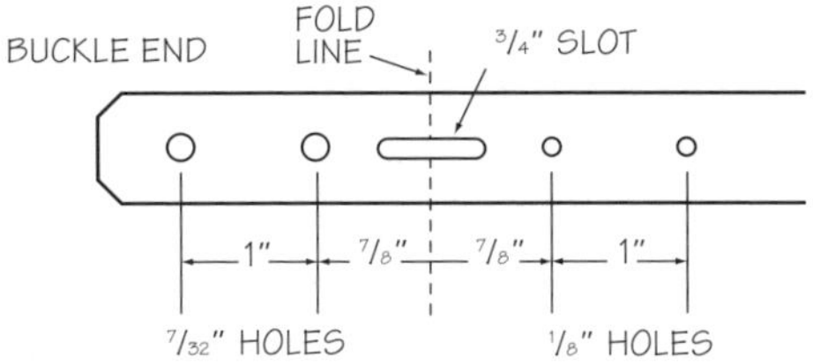

Step 4—Mark, then punch holes for, the billet end of the belt. Trim the billet end of the belt to a point.

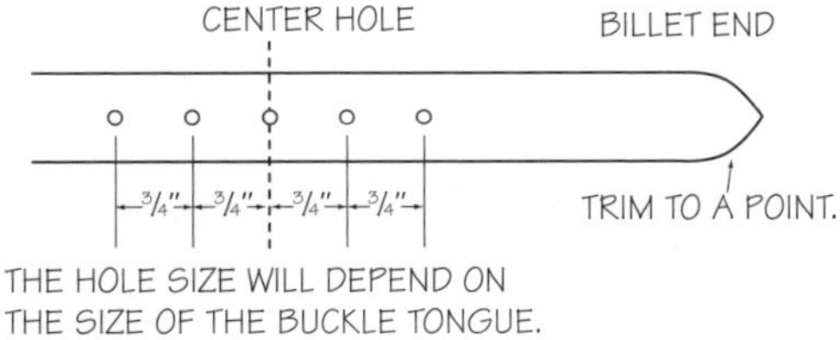

Step 5—Dress the edges of the belt.

Step 6—Attach belt snaps to the buckle end of the belt.

Step 7—Stamp and/or carve a design on the belt. If a name is to be stamped or carved, center it halfway between the tip of the buckle tongue and the center hole in the billet end. **Note:** The buckle end of the belt should face to the left when laid flat and stamping a name.

Step 8—Apply a dye or stain (if desired) and a leather finish.

Step 9—Attach the buckle to the buckle end of the belt to complete.

Making a Belt Keeper

Step 1—Cut a 6- to 7-inch long by 3/4-inch-wide strip of 4- to 5-ounce tooling leather. Fold the strip around two thicknesses of the belt. Trim the excess leather.

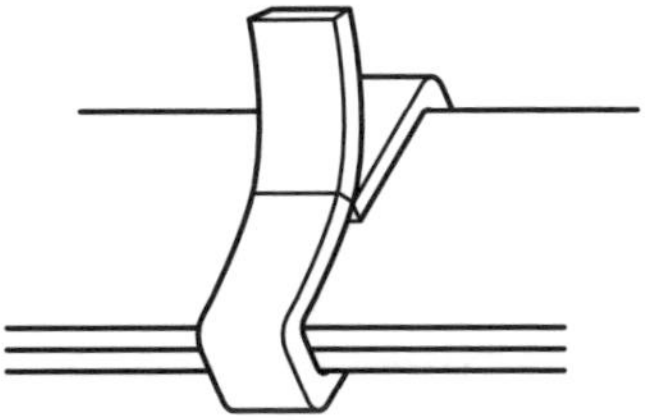

Step 2—Dress the edges, then stitch or staple the ends of the keeper together. Color it to match the belt, then apply a leather finish. Slide the keeper in place between the folded buckle end of the belt and fasten the snaps to secure.

Make a Knife Pouch

If you want, make the optional miniflashlight holder to be attached to the knife pouch. This project will use the following techniques:

- Cutting
- Punching holes
- Forming
- Hand-stitching
- Setting a snap fastener
- Dressing edges

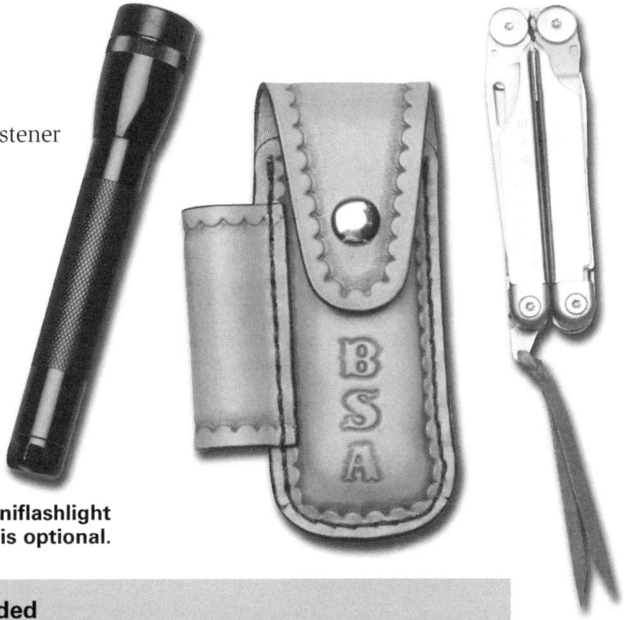

The miniflashlight holder is optional.

Materials Needed

- ☐ General leatherworking tools and supplies (See the beginning of this chapter.)
- ☐ One 6-by-12-inch piece of 4- to 5-ounce vegetable-tanned cowhide
- ☐ A stitching needle and 2 yards of waxed thread
- ☐ One line 24 snap fastener and setter
- ☐ 1/16-inch hole punch
- ☐ 5/32-inch hole punch
- ☐ Tools for stamping and/or carving designs (optional)
- ☐ Choice of dyes or stains (optional)
- ☐ Leather finish

CUTTING PATTERNS FOR THE KNIFE POUCH (ACTUAL SIZE)

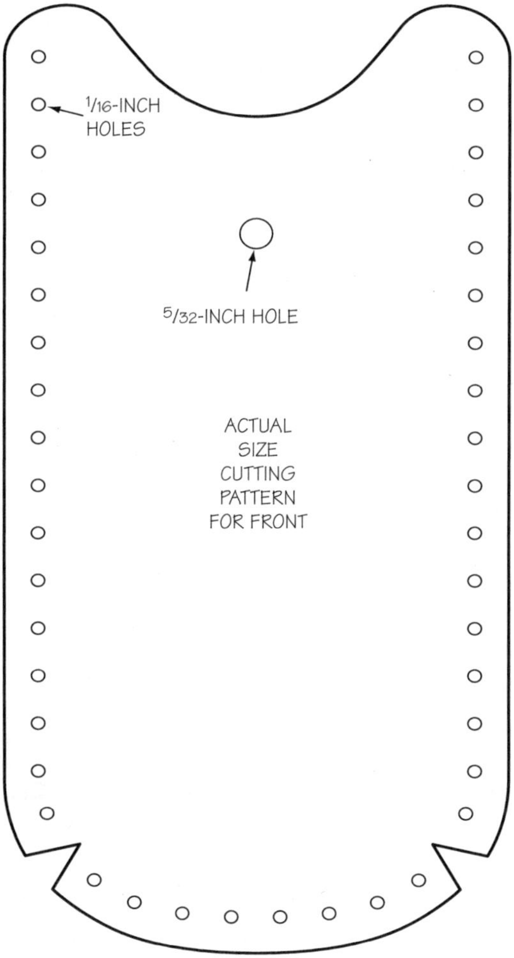

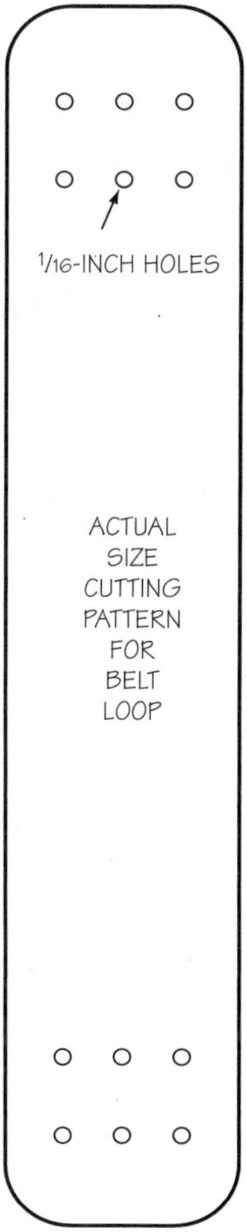

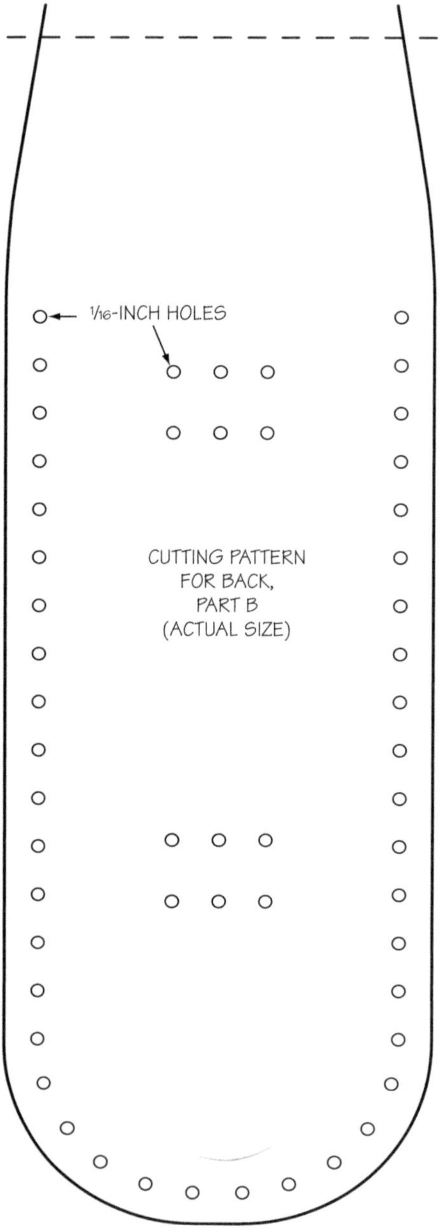

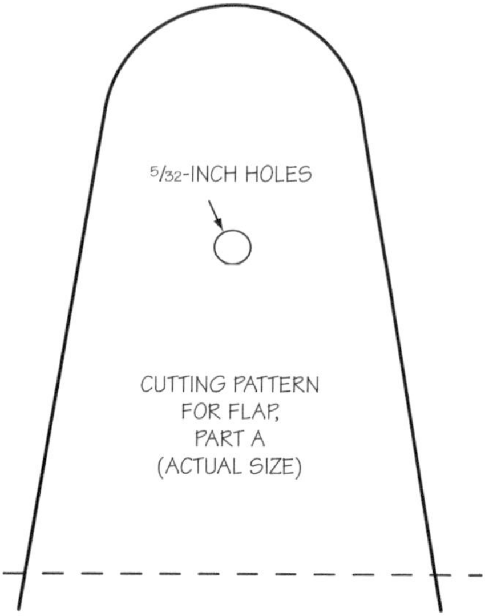

Instructions for these patterns:

The back/flap pattern is too big to fit this page, so you will need to connect parts A and B at the dotted line, as shown here, to complete the pattern.

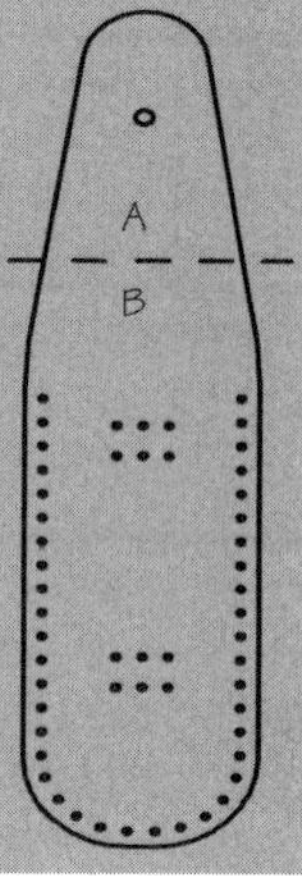

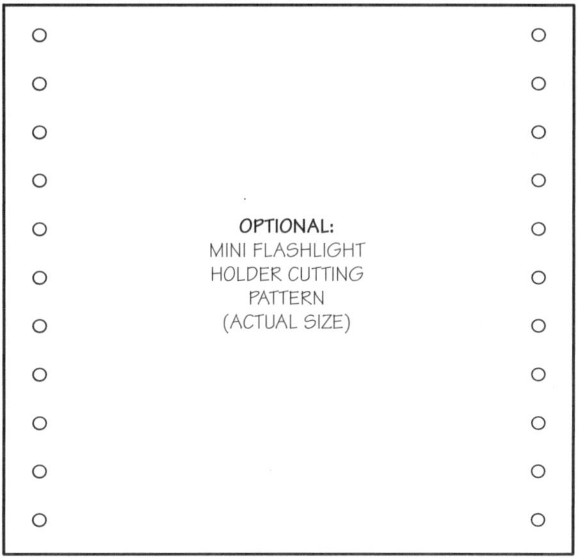

Assembling the Knife Pouch

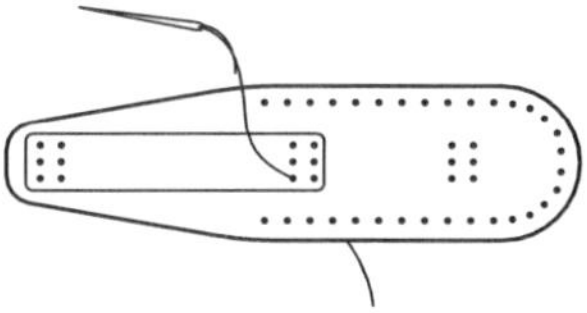

Before starting assembly, set the stud and eyelet part of the line 24 snap in the snap hole punched in the front part of the knife pouch. Set the cap and socket parts of the snap in the snap hole punched in the flap portion of the back part.

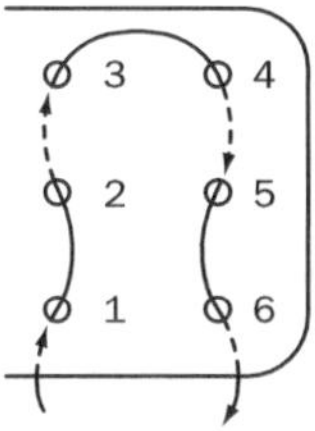

Step 1—To attach the belt loop, put the grain (smooth) sides of the belt loop and back/flap parts together, aligning the holes in one end of the loop with the top set of holes in the back part.

Step 2—Mentally number the holes 1 through 6. With half a yard of waxed thread, come up through hole 1 to the top side of the leather, leaving about 3 inches of thread on the underside. Then go down through hole 2, back up through 3, down through 4, up through 5, and down through 6.

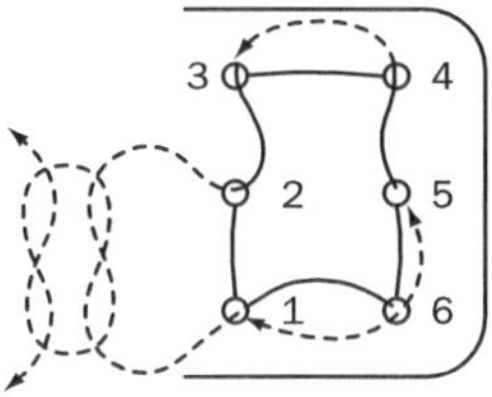

Step 3—From hole 6, come up through hole 1. Go down through 6, up through 5, down through 4, up through 3, and down through 2. Tie the thread ends in a knot to secure. Tap the knot flat with a mallet.

Step 4—Fold the belt loop part back and align the holes in the other end of the loop to the bottom set of holes in the back part, with the flesh (rough) side of the strap on the grain side of the back part. Stitch on the belt loop as explained in steps 1 and 2.

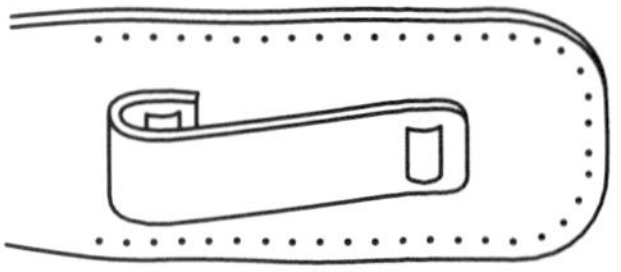

Note: Before stitching the knife pouch together, lightly dampen the flesh side of the front part with water. This will make it easier to form the front part to the back part. Stitch the pieces together while the leather is still damp.

Step 5—To stitch the front part to the back part, push the needle and 1½ yards of thread through the first hole in the back part, leaving 3 inches of thread at the end to tie off. Go through the second hole, then back through the first hole, then back through the second hole. Continue stitching in and out around the pouch.

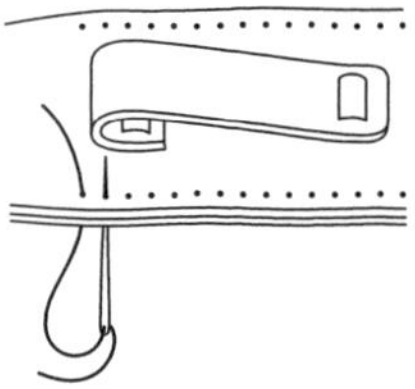

Step 6—There will be a notch between holes 17 and 18. Go through these holes twice, pulling the stitches tight to close up the notch and even the edges of the front and back parts. Repeat for the notch between holes 25 and 26.

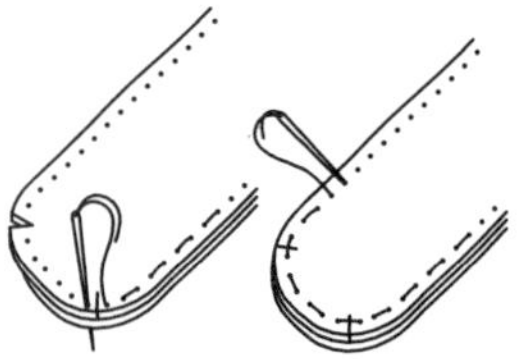

Step 7—Optional: If you want to add the flashlight holder, stop stitching when you reach the fourth hole past the second notch. In the bottom of the pouch, fold the hole-punched edges of the holder together, forming a loop. Sandwich the front and back parts of the pouch between the edges of the holder so the first holes in the bottom of the holder line up with the fourth hole past the second notch in the pouch. Continue stitching through all four layers of leather, securing the holder to the side of the pouch.

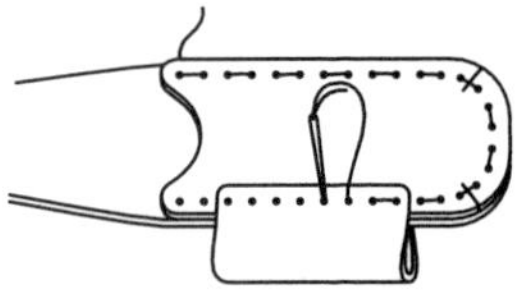

Step 8—When you have stitched completely around the pouch, stitch through the last two holes twice. Then, stitch back around the pouch, filling in alternate stitches. When you reach the beginning stitch, tie the ends of thread in a knot on the back side of the pouch. Trim the excess thread, then tap the knot flat with a mallet.

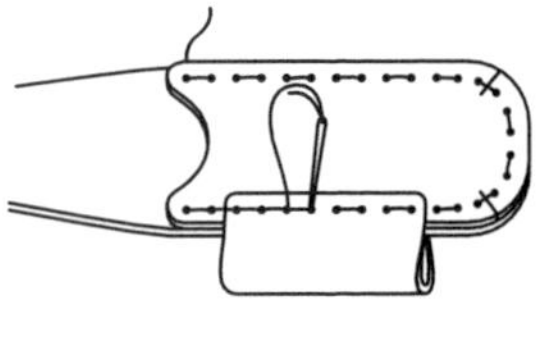

Make an Award Plaque

The award plaque will use the following techniques:

- Cutting
- Edge dressing
- Stamping and/or carving
- Coloring using dyes, stains, paints, or felt pens

Materials Needed

- ☐ General leatherworking tools and supplies (See the beginning of this chapter.)
- ☐ One 5-by-7-inch piece of 6- to 7-ounce. vegetable-tanned cowhide tooling leather
- ☐ Tools for stamping and/or carving designs
- ☐ Choice of dyes, stains, acrylic paints, permanent markers
- ☐ Leather finish

Getting Started

Step 1—Use the template provided to make a cardboard cutting pattern of the plaque.

Step 2—Using the pattern as a guide, transfer the shape of the plaque to the leather.

Step 3—Cut the plaque shape out of the leather.

Step 4—Stamp or carve a design on the leather as desired. Be sure to center the wording carefully before stamping.

Step 5—Apply a dye or stain (if desired) and a leather finish.

Step 6—For hanging, punch a hole in the top of the plaque.

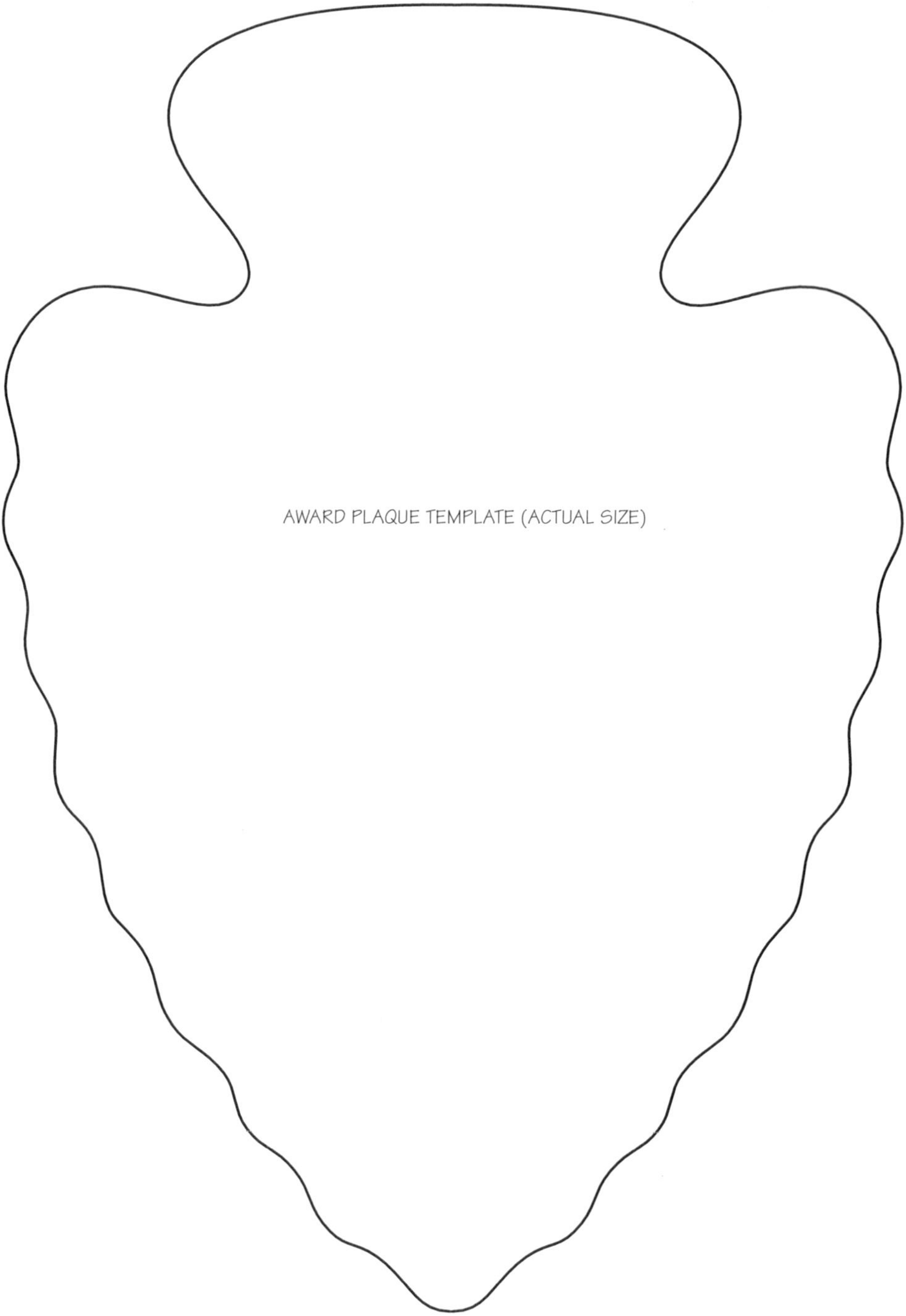

AWARD PLAQUE TEMPLATE (ACTUAL SIZE)

Award Plaque Design Ideas

Here are some ideas you can use to decorate your plaque. The design for the "1st place" plaque was created using the following tools:

- Center section—3/4-inch-block number stamp and 1/2-inch-block alphabet stamps
- Top and bottom—large star stamp
- Border—camouflage stamp
- Background—pear shader stamp

The designs shown here are not the actual size. Use the template provided for the actual size.

The "Camp Eagle" design was created using the following tools:

- Center section—1/2-inch-block alphabet stamps
- Border—veiner and camouflage stamp
- Top—eagle 3-D stamp and swivel knife to cut cloud
- Bottom—swivel knife to cut mountain (Use a modeling tool for details in the mountain and triangular-shaped carving tools for the trees.)

Materials Needed

- ☐ About three-quarters of a 1-square-foot of leather (The leather may be any soft, lightweight—3 to 5 ounces—suede or smooth finished leather such as cowhide, deer, elk, chamois, etc.)
- ☐ Two $1\frac{1}{2}$-yard lengths of $\frac{5}{32}$-inch lace for drawstrings (Leather boot or shoelaces will work.)
- ☐ 2 yards waxed thread or artificial sinew and a stitching needle
- ☐ $\frac{1}{16}$-inch hole punch
- ☐ $\frac{3}{16}$-inch hole punch
- ☐ Acrylic paints and/or permanent markers for decorating (optional)

Make a Fringed Pouch

The fringed pouch will use the following techniques:

- Cutting and making the fringe
- Hand-stitching
- Coloring using acrylic paints and/or permanent markers

CUTTING PATTERN FOR FRINGE (REDUCED)

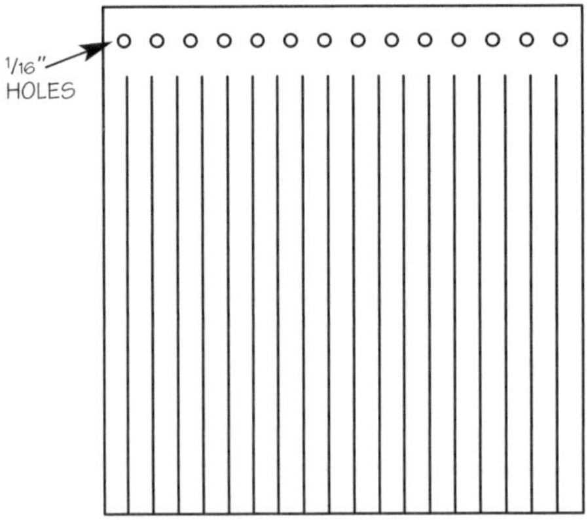

Important: **The fringe pattern must be enlarged 133 percent on a scanner or copier. The finished size should measure close to 3 $\frac{9}{16}$ inches wide by 3 $\frac{3}{4}$ inches high.**

CUTTING PATTERN FOR LEATHER POUCH (REDUCED), FRONT AND BACK

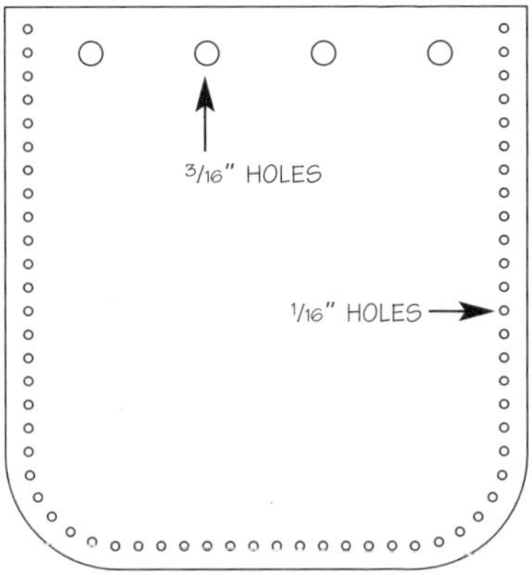

Important: **The pattern for the leather pouch must be enlarged 133 percent on a scanner or copier. The finished size should measure close to 5 $\frac{5}{8}$ inches wide by 6 inches deep.**

Getting Started

Step 1—Trace the cutting pattern for the fringe on the fringe piece, and mark where the holes will be punched. Then, cut the fringe and punch the holes (using the 1/16-inch hole punch) on the leather according to the pattern.

Step 2—Put the two pouch pieces together with the wrong side out and the right (finished) side in. Before stitching, center the fringe piece toward the inside, between the front and back pieces of the pouch.

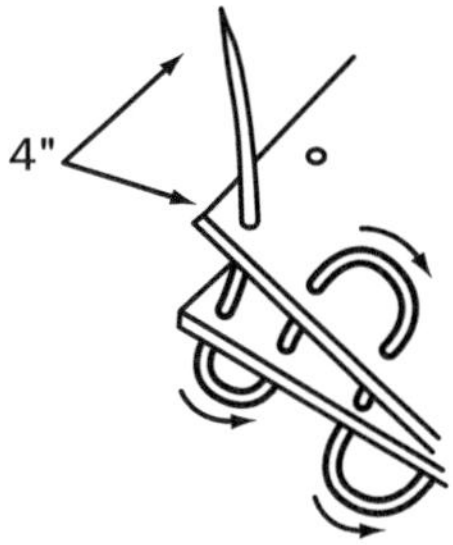

Step 3—Leaving a tail of 4 inches as you thread through the first hole, sew around the pouch in a running stitch. Make two stitches and then pull snug. Continue sewing all the way around the three sides, pulling the stitches snug as you go, leaving the top of the pouch open. Be sure to sew through the fringe at the bottom of the pouch.

Step 4—At the last stitch, turn the pouch over and, using the same running stitch, sew back to the starting point by filling in the opposite side of the first stitches.

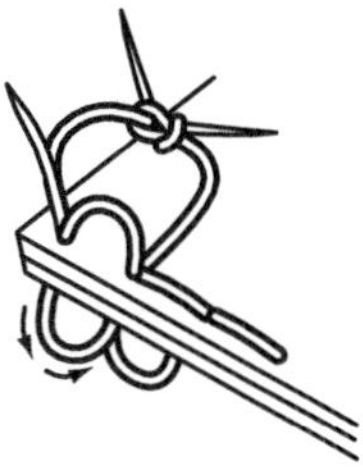

Step 5—Pull the last stitches tight and tie the ends together in a square knot.

Making the Drawstring

Fold one drawstring in half and tie an overhand knot, leaving a 1-inch loop in the center. With the loop outside the pouch, insert both ends of the drawstring inside the pouch through holes 1 and 2, then tie a square knot tightly against the inside seam. Lace in and out of the holes to the other end, and tie the ends together using an overhand knot. Starting from the opposite end that you began the first drawstring, lace the second drawstring in the same manner. Pull the drawstring loops to open the pouch and pull the opposite ends to close the pouch.

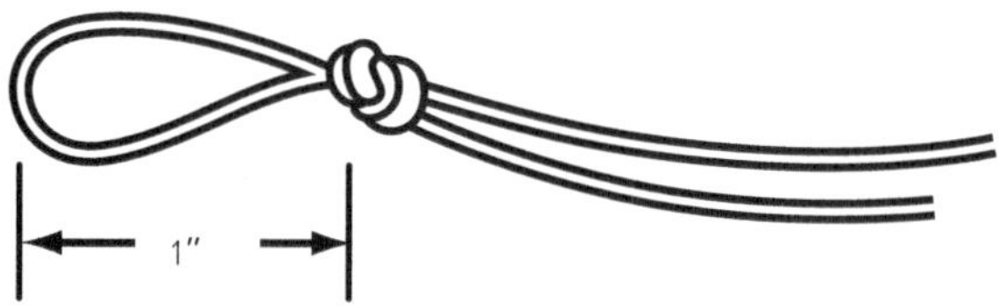

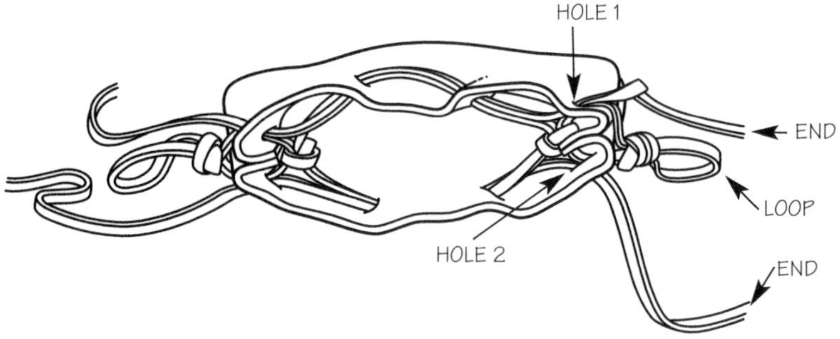

Patterns for Decorating the Fringed Pouch

Here are some patterns (actual size) for decorating your fringed pouch—or use your own designs. Carefully trace your pattern on the fringed pouch, then complete your project using acrylic paints and permanent ink markers, which are easy to use and dry quickly.

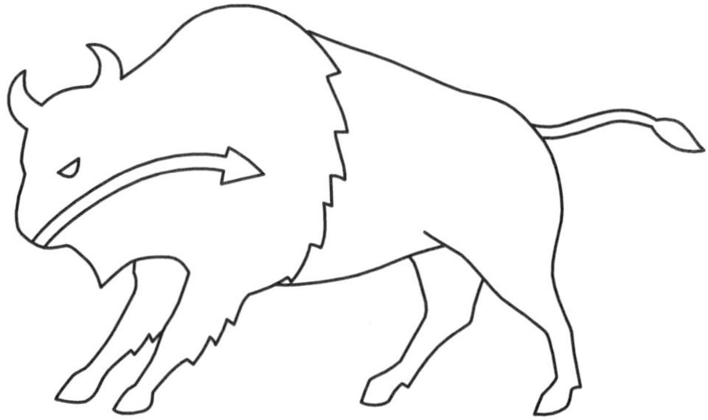

Braiding

Another popular type of leather crafting involves the braiding technique. Once you master this technique, you can make all kinds of things, including the lanyard described in the following steps.

Tips on Braiding

- Pull all strands tight. This will make the braid neat and uniform.
- If you must lay aside an unfinished braid, put paper clips on the loose strands or tie them in place with an overhand knot.
- Avoid twisting strands. They should lie flat and follow the circular contour of the braid.
- This table shows the lengths of lace necessary for braiding:

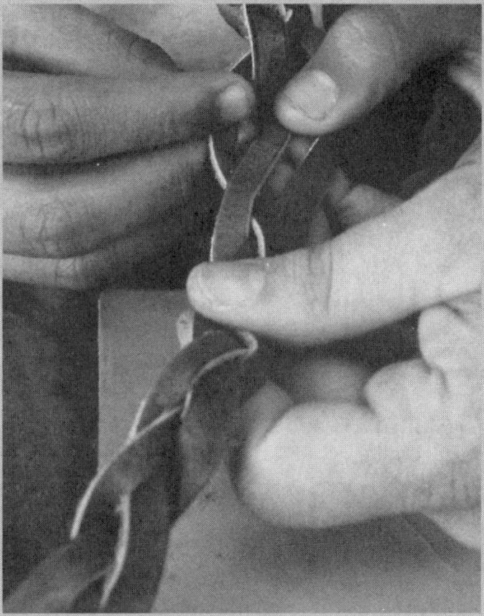

For the Round Braid

- Two strands of lace, each 3 feet long, will make 1 foot braided.
- Two strands of lace, each 6 feet long, will make 2 feet braided.
- Two strands of lace, each 9 feet long, will make 3 feet braided.

For the Square and Spiral Braids

- Two strands of lace, each 3 feet long, will make 4 inches braided.
- Two strands of lace, each 6 feet long, will make 8 inches braided.
- Two strands of lace, each 9 feet long, will make 12 inches braided.

Making the Lanyard

You will use the round braid, square braid, and the terminal Turk's head braiding techniques to make a lanyard. Begin with the **round braid:**

Materials Needed

- ☐ Two strands of 1/8-inch lace, each 3 1/2 yards long, in different colors
- ☐ One swivel snap
- ☐ One nail

Step 1—Draw the two strands evenly through the eye of the swivel snap and hang the snap on a nail.

Step 2—Arrange the strands as shown, and number them 1 through 4 from left to right.

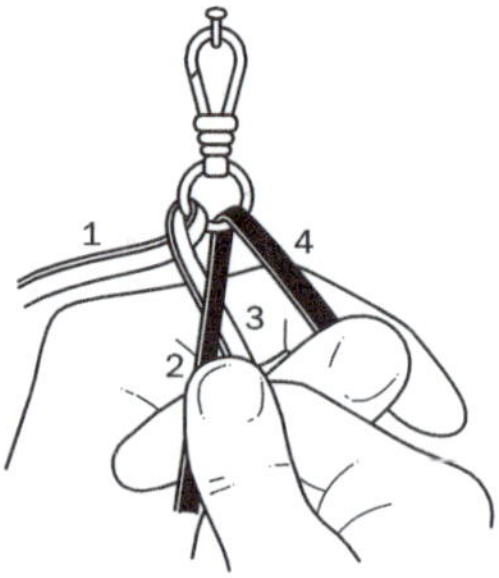

Step 3—Hold center strands 2 and 3 with the forefinger and thumb of your right hand. Grasp strand 4 with your left hand.

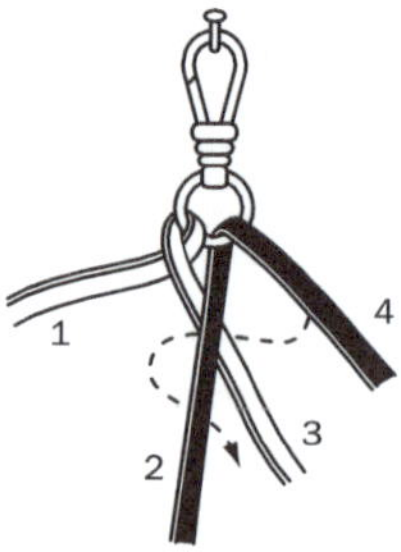

Step 4—Bring strand 4 to the front between strands 1 and 2.

Step 5—Bring strand 4 over strand 2 so that it lies parallel to strand 3. Draw all strands tight.

Step 6—Hold strands 2 and 4 with the forefinger and thumb of your left hand. Grasp strand 1 with a tight hand.

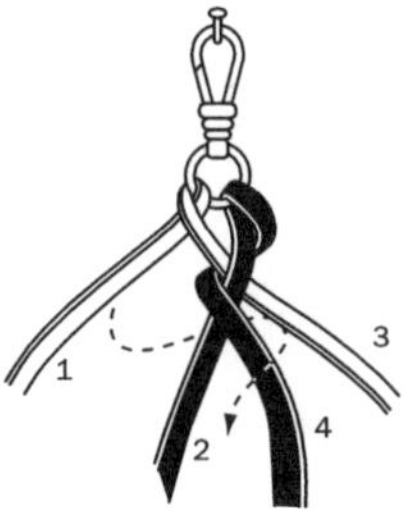

Step 7—Bring strand 1 forward between strands 3 and 4.

Step 8—Fold strand 1 over strand 4 so it lies parallel to strand 2. Draw all strands tight. Repeat steps 3 through 8 until the braid is 12 inches long.

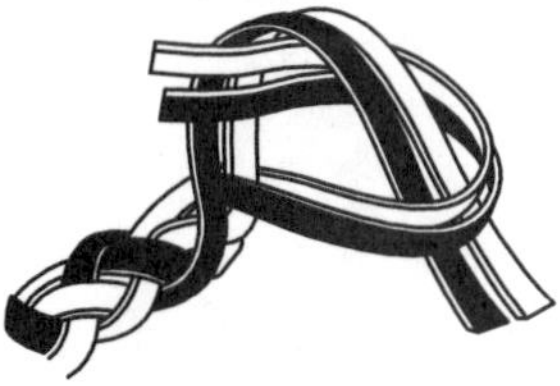

Step 9—End the round braid with an overhand knot. Hold the braid in your left hand, and tie the two left strands over the two right strands.

Now switch to the **square braid:**

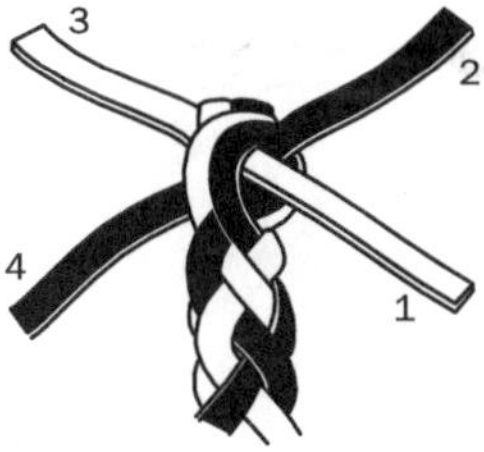

Step 10—Hold the lanyard upside-down in your left hand. Renumber strands as shown.

Step 11—Fold strand 1 over strand 2, leaving a small loop in strand 1. Hold the braid with the forefinger of your left hand. Repeat the same hold position after each step.

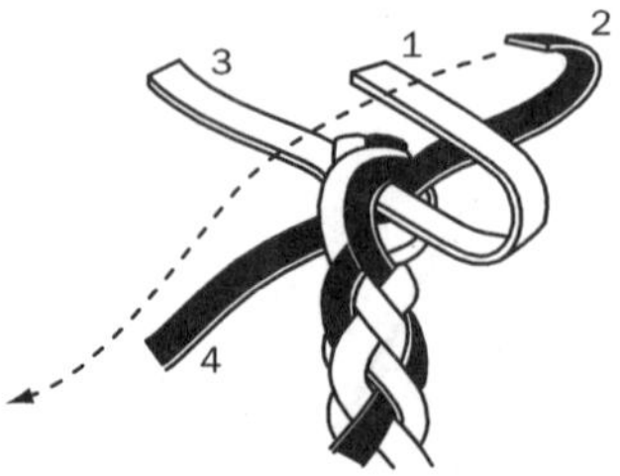

Step 12—Fold strand 2 over strand 1.

Step 13—Fold strand 3 over strand 2.

Step 14—Fold strand 4 over strand 3 and through loop from the beginning of the project.

Step 15—Leave the stitch slightly loose.

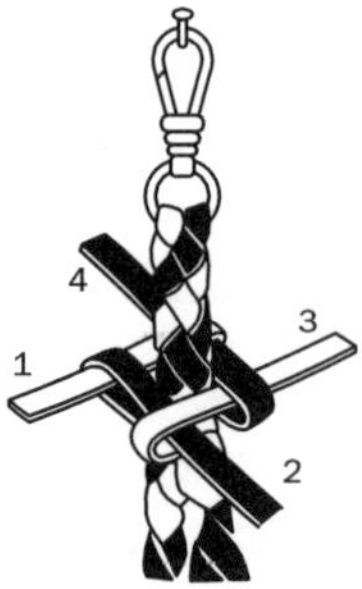

Step 16—Form the loop of the lanyard by folding the braid back and tucking it through the center of the last square braid. Tighten. Continue the square braid, with the lanyard as the core, until the remaining strands are 4 inches long.

Finish with the **terminal Turk's head:**

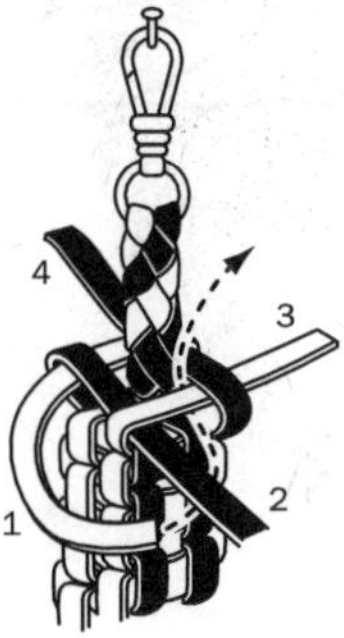

Step 17—Leave the last stitch of square braid loose. Renumber the strands as shown in step 16. Bring strand 1 under strand 2 and up through center. Leave the strands loose.

Step 18—Bring strand 2 under strand 3 and up through the center.

Step 19—Bring strand 3 under strand 4 and up through the center.

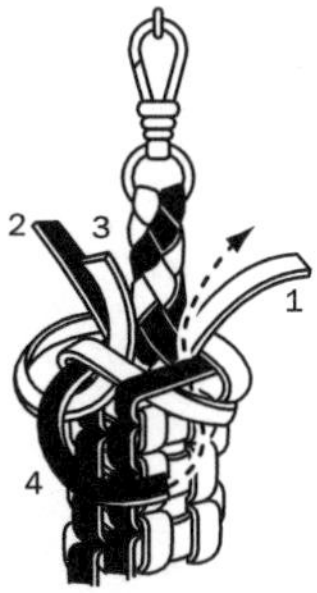

Step 20—Bring strand 4 under strand 1 and strand 2 up through the center. Tighten all strands starting with strand 1. Remember the terminal Turk's head should slide over the lanyard easily.

Step 21—Clip the end of the strand, leaving a tassel of about 1 inch.

Make the Mystery Braid Wristband or Belt

The mystery braid is a fun and fascinating technique that gives your wristband or belt an interesting effect.

Materials Needed

- ☐ General leatherworking tools and supplies (See the beginning of this chapter.)
- ☐ A length of 4- to 5-ounce leather (vegetable-tanned cowhide, suede, latigo, etc.), 1 1/8 inches wide for the wristband and wider for the belt
- ☐ Belt, glove, or line 20 snap
- ☐ 1/2-inch hole punch and snap setter

Making the Mystery Braid Wristband

Step 1—Measure around your wrist and add 3 inches. This is the length of leather you will need for a $1^1/_8$-inch-wide wristband.

Step 2—Punch the snap holes, trim the ends, and cut two even slits as shown in the illustration (forming three equal strands).

Step 3—Set the snaps as shown in the illustration. **Note:** When setting the snap, remember that the rounded end of the band will snap *over* the squared end.

Step 4—Decorate as desired, apply the edge dressing, and then the leather finish.

Step 5—Follow the instructions for mystery braiding later in this chapter.

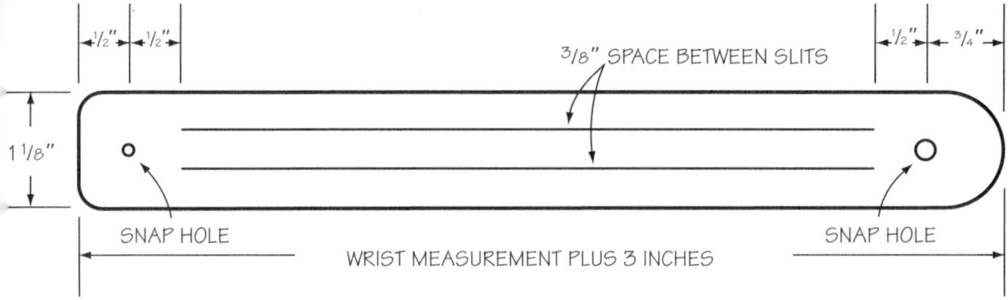

Making the Mystery Braid Belt

Step 1—Cut a belt strip as explained in "Make a Belt" earlier in this chapter, but *add approximately 1 inch to the length of the waist for every 12-inch section to be braided.* So, for a 24-inch braided section, add 2 inches to the length of the leather you will need.

> **Materials Needed for the Belt**
>
> Refer to the "Make a Belt" project earlier in this book. However, see step 2 to get the correct length.

Step 2—Cut two even slits (forming three 1/2-inch-wide strands for a typical 1 1/2-inch-wide belt) in the belt strip, as shown. Remember to leave plenty of room at both ends of the belt strip for the buckle tongue slot, snap holes, and billet holes. **Note:** So that the size can be adjusted if necessary, do not mark or punch the holes until after the belt has been braided.

Step 3—Trim the billet end to a point. Do all decorating and edge dressing, then apply a leather finish.

Step 4—Follow the instructions for mystery braiding later in this chapter.

Step 5—Lay the braided belt strip out flat and remeasure to establish the correct waist size. Mark, then punch the buckle tongue slot, snap holes, and billet holes. Attach a belt keeper, if desired, and a buckle to complete the project.

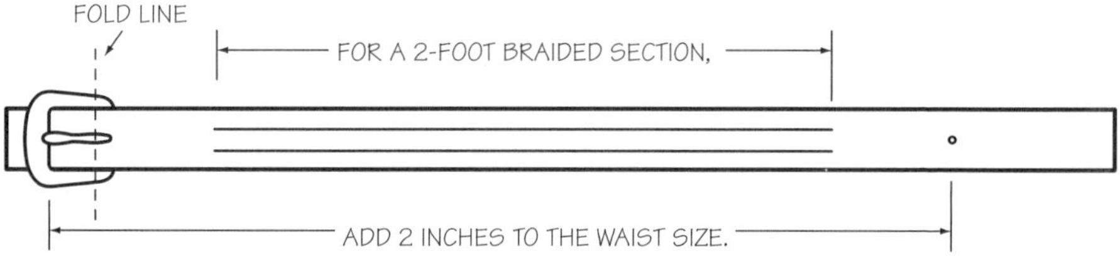

How to Do the Mystery Braid

Use these instructions for both the wristband and the belt.

Step 1—Hold the strip with the rounded end at the top and the flat end at the bottom (see figure 1).

Step 2—Bring the bottom end of the strip up between strands 2 and 3 (see figure 2), and adjust and push the resulting twist to the bottom.

Step 3—Bring the bottom end of the strip up again, then pass strand 1 over 2, then 3 over 1, and 2 over 3. Pass the bottom end of the strip between strands 2 and 3 (see figure 3). Adjust and work the braid up to the top of the strip. *This completes the first braid cycle.*

Step 4—To complete a second braid cycle, pass the bottom end of the strip between strands 2 and 3 (see the dashed arrow in figure 4). As in step 3, pass strand 1 over 2, 3 over 1, and 2 over 3, then pass the bottom end of the strip between strands 2 and 3. Straighten the braids. *This completes two braid cycles.* To continue braiding more cycles, follow step 3 until the strands are too short to complete another full cycle. Adjust the strands so that all the braids are even.

FIG. 1

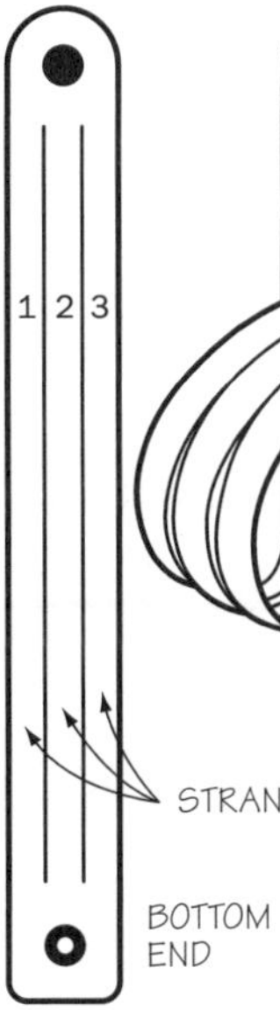

FIG. 2

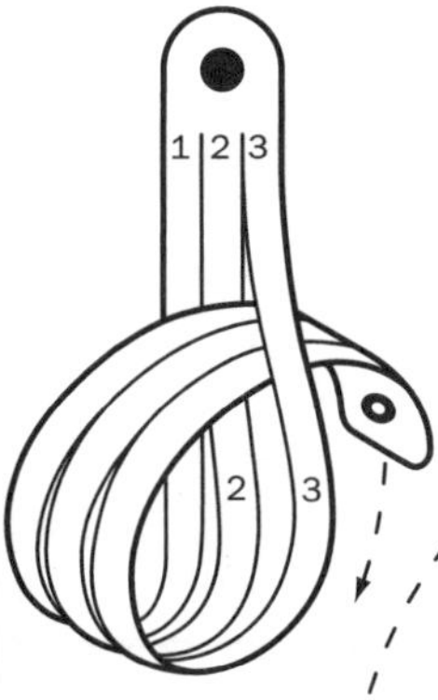

FIG. 3

FIG. 4

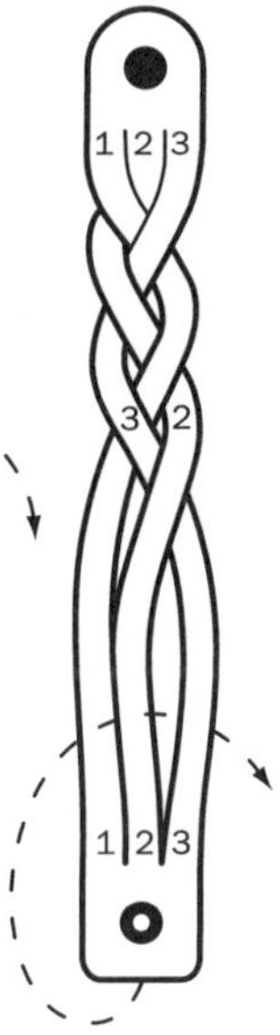

Leather Care

Leather is one of nature's most durable materials. Modern tanning methods contribute to its natural durability by adding oils, waxes, and other ingredients that soften and help preserve the leather.

Leather that has been neglected will feel dry and stiff to the touch. This is because oils in the leather have dried. To restore the leather, these oils must be replaced.

Cleaning and Reconditioning

Clean leather before applying a reconditioner (or conditioner):

Step 1—Use a brush to remove any loose dirt.

Step 2—Clean the leather thoroughly with saddle soap or other leather cleaner, following the manufacturer's instructions.

Step 3—Allow the leather to dry completely before reconditioning.

Many good conditioners are available, including mink and neat's-foot oils. Work the conditioner into the leather until the softness and pliability returns. Most of these substances will darken the leather, which in most cases will enhance the leather's appearance.

Caring for Leather Goods

Normal weather conditions and use can have harmful effects on leather items if they do not receive proper care. Be sure to follow these tips after using leather items.

Outdoor Gear. For items such as hiking boots, baseball gloves, and saddle tack, reconditioning usually is sufficient to give some degree of water resistance. Water-repellent coatings for leather are available if necessary.

Dress Shoes. Using oil-type conditioners will make the shoes impossible to shine. Instead of oil, apply a good quality shoe polish after cleaning the leather. Allow the polish to dry, then buff to a high gloss with a shoe brush or soft cloth.

Suede Articles. Suede should be cleaned and reconditioned with products specifically made for use on suede. Using products intended for smooth leathers on suede may damage the suede's fuzzy surface texture.

Fine Leathers. Leave the cleaning and reconditioning of fine leather articles, such as furniture and clothing, to trained professionals.

Leather Tanning

Tanning is the process of converting the hide or skin of an animal into leather. The two most popular ways of doing this are vegetable tanning and mineral or chrome tanning.

Vegetable Tanning

The basic element used is tannic acid, derived from the bark or leaves of certain trees, shrubs, or other plants. Only vegetable-tanned leather will retain the designs made by carving or stamping. It may also be molded into almost any shape after being dampened with water, and it will hold that shape after it dries.

Mineral or Chrome Tanning

The basic element used is potassium bichromate. Leather that has been chrome tanned is normally soft to the touch, pliable, and somewhat water-repellent. This makes it unsuitable to be carved or stamped. Cut edges of this leather may appear bluish green, a color left by minerals used in the tanning process. Leather tanned by this method is made into clothing, furniture, automobile upholstery, and many other items that call for a soft, durable leather.

The Tannery Operation

When hides arrive at the tanner, they are temporarily preserved by salting like beef jerky or by drying to prevent rotting. When the hides are needed, they are first washed to rehydrate and to remove any salt.

Then comes dehairing. After soaking in a large vat of limewater to loosen the hairs and a thorough rinsing, the hides are ready for tanning. If they are dried at this point, they make rawhide, such as is used in a rawhide mallet or dog bones.

Tanning, the next step, is where the hide collagen is chemically converted from rawhide into leather, which can then be dried and used without being too stiff and without rotting. Both these operations require careful control of chemicals.

Tanning has been done historically in vats in the ground using vegetable-tanning materials. This step used to take up to a year, but is done in modern times in about a month. Modern chrome tanning, developed only in the late 1800s, is performed in large rotating drums in a day's time.

After the tanning, the leather is washed and dyed if needed. Then the oils—"fat liquors"—are worked into the leather, depending on its intended use. A tooling leather will have a small amount of light oil so it may be carved and stamped; harness leather will have a great deal of heavy tallow to make it waterproof. The leather is then wrung (hand-wringing is still the best method), and laid smooth either by hand rubbing or on a setting-out machine. Lastly, the leather is allowed to dry.

Many modern leathers are finished by sanding then painting the surface. This type of leather goes into shoes, car seats, and shiny clothes. Many other leathers, such as tooling and saddle leathers, retain the original beauty of their grain surface. Look closely, and you will see a scar or a wrinkle just as you see on your own skin.

Remember to take care of your leather as you would your skin, by washing it if it gets too dirty, and by giving it a little oil (but not too much) every now and again. Leather will last forever if you take good care of it.

How to Tan the Skin of a Small Animal

The skins of small animals may be tanned or cured successfully by Scouts, but amateurs should never destroy animals for this purpose. It takes an expert to handle valuable furs. Furthermore, it would be contrary to the spirit of Scouting to hunt harmless animals merely to obtain a few skins.

Small wild animal skins suitable for tanning are rabbits, squirrels, prairie dogs, and groundhogs. You can obtain such skins from slaughterhouses, farmers, or ranchers. Skins occasionally are available from dealers in furs and hides or from farmers and others who trap predatory animals. During the hunting season, Scout troops that want to undertake larger tanning or leatherwork projects may be able to obtain the skins of some larger animals such as deer or elk from hunters.

Curing a Skin

Curing is the process of completely drying a skin; the hair is not removed.

Step 1—The first step is to clean off any flesh or fatty particles that remain after the animal is skinned.

Step 2—Draw the skin over a board, flesh side out. The board should be big enough so that the skin can be kept stretched to its original size while drying.

Step 3—Rub salt into the skin to absorb the moisture. Pay particular attention to the edges; the salt will prevent flies from laying eggs in the outer edges.

Step 4—Drying is best done in the open air in the shade. Avoid fire and the heat of the sun; freezing may cause the skin to crack. A uniform temperature is best. It may be necessary to keep the skin indoors in rainy or very hot or cold weather. The time it takes for the skin to dry completely will vary according to the weather and size of the skin. During the drying process, additional salt should be applied occasionally to help absorb the moisture. The skin may be tacked to a floor, a wall, or an inclined board. Store dry hides in a cool place until ready to tan.

Dehairing a Skin

The first step in tanning is to remove the hair from a skin. This may be done with a limewater solution.

Step 1—If the skin has been cured or dried, soak it with water to soften before putting it in the solution.

Step 2—Make a milk-of-lime solution by mixing 2 pounds, about 1 cup at a time, of unslaked lime into 1 gallon of water. Stir the mixture carefully, adding small quantities of lime at a time so that it will not boil out or splash on hands or clothing. The solution can cause burns.

Step 3—Handling the skin with sticks or paddles and wearing rubber gloves, immerse the moist skin in the solution. Let it stand for about an hour, then test at frequent intervals. The skin is ready when the hair slips.

Step 4—Remove the skin and rinse with at least 1 gallon of clear water, depending on the size of the skin. Repeat three or four times.

Step 5—After the hair is loosened and while the skin is still wet, it should be scraped. One Scout may hold the skin taut across a 2-by-4 or nail it to a workbench. A wide putty knife or similar blunt-edged tool makes an effective scraper—hold it at a slant, and have the second Scout push or pull the skin with sufficient pressure to pull the hair from it in progressive strokes. If it is impossible to remove all the hair in one operation, leave the skin soaking in clear water until the dehairing can be completed.

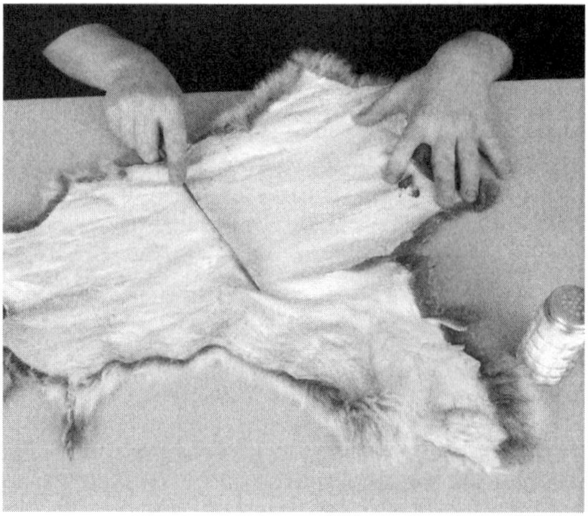

Step 6—Note that a thin skin still covers the surface. This is known as a "scarf skin," and it reveals the characteristic grain of the leather. Much of the strength of the leather is in this grain surface, and it must be retained if leather articles are to be made from it. If a soft or suede finish is desired, this surface skin is removed by continued scraping while the skin is still moist. The tanning process should follow immediately. If this is not possible, the skin must be kept wet overnight. **Note:** The hair of a freshly skinned deer hide will slip or loosen sufficiently to permit scraping after a few hours of soaking in lukewarm water.

Salt-Alum Tanning

The salt-alum process, an old method of fur-skin tanning, is still widely used. It usually produces skins with stretch and flexibility.

A salt-alum tanning solution may be made as follows:

Step 1—Dissolve 1 pound of ammonia alum or potash alum in 1 gallon of water.

Step 2—Dissolve 2 ounces of washing soda (crystallized sodium carbonate) and 8 ounces of shale in 1/2 gallon of water.

Step 3—When it is dissolved, slowly and constantly pour and stir the soda-salt solution into the alum solution.

A cleaned and softened skin may be tanned by immersion in this solution from two to five days, depending upon its thickness. Because of the action of alum on some furs, it may be best to apply the tanning liquor as a paste to the flesh side only.

Step 4—Mix the tanning liquor with sufficient flour to make a thin paste. Add the flour in small quantities with a little water and mix thoroughly to avoid lumps.

Step 5—Tack the skin out smoothly, flesh side up. Apply a coating of the paste carefully, at intervals of a day, from two to three coatings, depending upon the thickness of the skin. Only thick skins should need as many as three treatments. Leave the last coating on for three to four days.

Step 6—Scrape off the coating and rinse the skin clean in clear water, putting in about an ounce of borax to a gallon of water. Finally, rinse in water only.

Step 7—Work the skin over a beam to remove most of the water, stretch it out flat, and sponge over the flesh side with a thin sap paste. Let the paste completely soak in, apply a thin coat of oil, then rinse, stretch into shape, and hang up dry.

Large commercial tanning vats

Leather-Related Businesses

An optional requirement for the Leatherwork merit badge is to visit and report on a leather-related business. Almost every town in America has a leather-related business available to tour. Whether it's a small, custom-leather shop or a large industry (tannery, apparel manufacturer, etc.), it will be exciting to explore the endless ways leather is used today.

You may be surprised how welcome you will be in these industries. Most shop or factory managers will be pleased to give you the "grand tour" and answer questions about their operation. Try to get an overall understanding of exactly what takes place; take notes and pictures (but ask first, please).

Touring the Business

Here are some good questions to ask:

1. What kind of products do they make or sell?
2. What kinds of leathers do they use?
3. Is the leather hand-tooled, machine-embossed, sewn, or laced?
4. Who buys the products? Are they sold directly to the general public or to other businesses?
5. How many hides of leather are used each month or year?

6. Where does the leather come from?
7. What supplies are used on the leather (tools, dyes, finishes)?
8. How long has the business been in operation?
9. How many employees work there?

The more questions you ask, the more knowledgeable you will become. Perhaps, some day, you will be employed by a business related to the leather industry. The opportunities are many and varied. Take the time to observe and you will learn that leather touches almost every part of our lives.

Where to Go

Here are just a few businesses related to the leather industry that may be located near you or worth a trip as a troop:

- A leathercraft or general craft retail store will offer a wide variety and source for samples, techniques, and history of leatherwork. Ask to speak to the manager about what leather items, supplies, and instructional materials they sell. To locate such a shop, look in your local telephone directory under the headings "leather" or "crafts."
- Leather tanneries are located nationwide. Call for an appointment and a troop tour of the facility. You will be able to see firsthand the manufacturing of leather from start to finish.
- Saddleries, farm and ranch supply stores, and boot and shoe repair shops are found everywhere. Many can arrange on-site demonstrations about leather care, maintenance, and repair. Managers will be happy to offer helpful techniques.
- Manufacturers of custom leather products (leather-covered furniture, home furnishings, upholstery) use a variety of leather, tooling, staining, and finishing techniques in today's homes, automobiles, and recreational vehicles.
- Related industries to leatherwork will include makers of leatherwork tools, dyes, and finishes. Sources can be located through leathercraft retail stores.

Glossary

bovine. An ox, cow, or similar animal.

carving. Putting a design on the surface of leather using a swivel knife and other leathercraft tools.

casing (cased). Properly moistening the leather prior to carving and stamping designs on the surface.

chrome tanning. A tanning process that uses chemicals containing chromium salts to convert the raw hides into leather. The hides are usually colored and finished at the tannery to be made into finished goods.

full grain. The top layer of leather, wherein the surface has not been corrected and the hair follicles are visible; the strongest part of the hide.

grain. The markings (pattern, grain, or texture) on the side of leather from which the hair has been removed. The markings or texture can be natural or man-made.

hair-on. Leather that is fully tanned, with the hair or fur left on.

hide. Full animal skin (usually cows or other large animals).

oil tanning. The process of tanning with animal oils, which is used in the manufacture of certain soft leathers, particularly chamois and certain kinds of buckskin. Fish oil is generally used.

ounces. Term used for measuring thickness of leather. One ounce is about $^{1}/_{64}$ inch thick. (Example: 8 ounces of leather is $^{8}/_{64}$ or $^{1}/_{8}$ inch thick.)

rawhide. Animal hide that has been cured but not tanned. Very hard and stiff. Becomes pliable when wet.

shearling. Leather made from short wool sheep or lamb skins, sheared before slaughter. The wool being left on the skin when tanned and used for such items as garments or slippers.

side. Half of a hide, usually of cows and other large bovines.

skins. Whole hides of smaller animals and calves.

split leather. The lower layer of leather, below the grain, not very strong. May be sueded or finished.

stamping. Putting a design on the surface of leather using (stamping) tools and a mallet (no swivel knife).

suede. Tanned leather that has been buffed or sanded to produce a nap (fuzzy surface texture).

tanning (tannage). The process of converting the hide or skin of an animal into leather.

thickness. Thickness of leather is measured in ounces. Each ounce equals 1/64 inch. An 8-ounce leather piece should be 8/64 (1/8) inch thick.

tooled. Term used to describe leather that has a design compressed into the surface by means of carving or stamping.

vegetable tanning. The tanning process that uses extracts from natural tree bark to convert the raw hides into leather. Often called tooling leather. Can be carved or stamped when wet.

Leathercraft Resources

Books

Burnett, Paul. *Basic Leatherwork.* The Leather Factory, 1986.

Grant, Bruce. *Encyclopedia of Rawhide and Leather Braiding.* Cornell Maritime Press, 1972.

Tandy Leather Co. *Lacing and Stitching for Leathercraft.* 1997.

Tandy Leather Co. *Leather Crafting.* 1998.

Michaels, Valerie. *The Leatherworking Handbok: A Practical Illustrated Source Book of Techniques and Projects.* Cassell PLC, 1995.

Moody, Ben. *Just Tooling Around: Easy-to-Do Leather Stamping.* Hot Off the Press, Inc., 1994.

Richards, Matt. *Deerskins into Buckskins: How to Tan with Natural Materials/ A Field Guide for Hunters and Gatherers.* Backcountry Publishing, 1997.

Stohlman, Al. *The Art of Making Leather Cases, Volume I.* Tandy Leather Company, 1979.

———. *The Art of Making Leather Cases, Volume II.* Tandy Leather Company, 1983.

———. *The Art of Making Leather Cases, Volume III.* Tandy Leather Company, 1987.

———. *Coloring Leather.* Tandy Leather Co., 1985.

———. *How to Carve Leather.* Tandy Leather Co., 1952.

———. *Leathercraft Tools (How to Use Them, How to Sharpen Them).* Tandy Leather Co., 1984.

Organizations and Web Sites

The Leather Factory

P.O. Box 50429
Fort Worth, TX 76105
Telephone: 817-496-4414
Toll-free telephone: 800-433-3201
Fax: 817-496-9806
Web site: *http://www.leatherfactory.com*

Tandy Leather Company

5882 East Berry Street
Fort Worth, TX 76119
Toll-free telephone: 888-890-1611
Fax: 817-451-5254
Web site: *http://www.tandyleather.com*

Acknowledgments

The Boy Scouts of America is grateful to the following people for their tireless and meticulous work on the revision of this merit badge pamphlet.

- Tony Laier, director of research and development, The Leather Factory and Tandy Leather Company; designer/artist for Steel Strike Leather Products
- Karen Holze Laier of The Leather Factory, Tandy Leather Company, and Steel Strike Leather Products
- Wray Thompson, chief executive officer, and Ron Morgan, president, The Leather Factory and Tandy Leather Company, Fort Worth, Texas
- L. Shepley Hermann, president, Hermann Oak Leather Company, St. Louis, Missouri

Photo Credits

Tom Copeland—cover, pages 12, 14, 21 (bottom), 65, 74, and 76

Daniel Giles—pages 6 and 7

Vince Heptig—page 13

Courtesy Hermann Oak Leather Company, St. Louis, Mo.—page 84

Courtesy Tony Laier—page 85

Brian Payne—pages 4, 5, 10, 77, 78, and 82

Randy Piland—page 11

All other photos are the property of the Boy Scouts of America.

The Boy Scouts of America is grateful to The Leather Factory and Tandy Leather Company for their unconditional support during the entire production of this new edition of the *Leatherwork* merit badge pamphlet. Their commitment to providing expertise, equipment, and other resources has made this new pamphlet possible.

LF

Tandy

LEATHER COMPANY®

EST. 1919

Notes